The Phoenix Marriage

God Creates Beauty Out of Ashes

Equip Your Marriage Ministries

Equip Your Marriage is a Christian ministry born out of the blood, sweat, and tears that Kyle and Tammy Gabhart have invested in making their marriage a testament to the love and grace of Jesus Christ.

Through this ministry we provide hope and healing to couples by utilizing a combination of online and offline resources, including books, videos, social media messages, and even one-on-on couples mentoring to walk out the marriage renewal process.

Follow us online:

 *www.EquipYourMarriage.com*

 *www.facebook.com/EquipYourMarriage*

 *@equip_marriage*

#PhoenixMarriage
#EquipYourMarriage

 *www.pinterest.com/EquipMarriage*

The Phoenix Marriage

KYLE GABHART

Your most important earthly relationship can be restored, renewed, and reborn.

God creates beauty out of ashes.

Edited by Jennifer L Hunt

Cover Design and Illustrations by Fistbump Media

Equip Your Marriage Ministries
Keller, Texas

Published in Keller, TX by Equip Your Marriage Ministries.

This title may be purchased in bulk for educational, business, fund-raising, or sales promotional use. For information, please e-mail EquipYourMarriage@gmail.com.

ISBN 978-0692266090

Printed in the United States of America

Acknowledgements

Lindsey Hartz – Thank you for your publishing and promotion coaching and overall encouragement.

Dan King and Fistbump Media – The book cover and illustrations are gorgeous. Thank you so much!

Jennifer Hunt – I cannot thank you enough. You are my editor, my friend, my sister in Christ, and my "Redeemer of Words." Thank you for your attention to detail, your passion for English, and your commitment to Biblical integrity. You are, indeed, an *Eshet Chayil*.

My parents – I'm not in prison, so you must have done something right. Thank you for your love and for always believing in me. I am living proof of Proverbs 22:6 because of you both.

My children – Thank you for allowing me the time to write this book and launch this ministry with Mom. It has gobbled up precious time, but you guys have been troopers. Thank you for sticking together even while I was falling apart. You guys are amazing. Each of you has a special purpose designed by God, and I am honored to help shape you on that path. Throughout your lives, hold tight to Micah 6:8. I love you all dearly.

My faith-filled wife, Tammy – Words fail to express how much you mean to me. Thank you for your love for Jesus. Thank you for loving me even when I was unlovable. You stood for our marriage when I was only willing to stand for myself. I am constantly in awe of your grace and Christlike love. Thank you for joining me on this crazy adventure and for loving me and the kiddos so selflessly. If they grow up to be half the person you are, then I'll consider it a success. I had no idea the full extent of God's favor in my life when He introduced me to you. But I realize now that He was entrusting me with His precious daughter. The broken road we have walked together hasn't been easy, but I'm glad I've walked it with you. You are my Jeremiah 29:11, my Proverbs 18:22, and my James 1:17. I love you.

Jesus – You are Grace. You are Love. I don't know why you put up with me, but thank you. I am blessed beyond measure. Thank you for redeeming my marriage and my family. I dedicate this book and the ministry of my family to making your name known. You are my everything.

Contents

Section I Up in Flames

Section II Rebuild, Renew, and Restore

Section III Beauty out of Ashes

Appendix

Preface

When my wife, Tammy, and I decided to rebuild our battered and torn marriage, we were surprised to discover very few viable resources. There were books on how to communicate better and books about sex. We found couple's devotionals, marriage conferences, weekend retreats, and a variety of other tools for improving or fine-tuning our relationship. To be fair, we found some resources that helped with pieces of the process, but nothing comprehensive. Tammy and I needed a holistic plan for establishing a firm foundation in our marriage, re-building trust, and dealing with the constant threats to our bond (both internal and external). Moreover, we wanted some sense of what the overall process would look like. We knew re-connecting with each other and refreshing our marriage would not be easy, but we had no way to gauge our progress and no idea what the tone or tempo of the healing would entail. It was scary and a bit intimidating, but we knew that through the power of Christ we could do anything (Philippians 4:13).

This book is our attempt at answering that void by providing a process through the pain. When a marriage is swallowed in darkness, we hope to light the way through. When a couple finds themselves at a crossroads of commitment, we want to offer insight into re-building the trust. When the flame is gone because the relationship has been burned, we want to provide a compassionate guide to reassure that God creates beauty out of ashes.

We hope this book can also serve as a wake-up call and a health-check for couples who have not reached their breaking point. No matter how long you have been married or how strong your bond might be, take heed. Given enough neglect, any marriage can be threatened and eventually destroyed. A relationship is a living organism, and it must be fed to keep it alive. Apathy will erode the fabric of your relationship as powerfully as an affair. It takes longer, but the end result is the same – a pile of rubble and ash.

Marriage isn't easy, but it is worth the effort. All you need is two willing partners, another couple or two to serve as mentors, and a commitment to do the work necessary to build communication skills and forge a deep and intimate bond. We have discovered any marriage is at risk of collapse if one or both partners stop investing in the relationship. Likewise, any marriage – no matter how badly damaged – can be restored and made to flourish through honesty, transparency, prayer, and persistent prioritization of the relationship. God can take that pile of ashes and create something beautiful. He delights in a good love story and He longs to redeem your marriage.

We pray that through this book your marriage is blessed, healed, and restored.

1

God Can Save ANY Marriage

And I will give them one heart and put a new spirit within them; I will remove their heart of stone from their bodies and give them a heart of flesh.

Ezekiel 11:19, HCSB

O N DECEMBER 16TH, 2012, my wife and I sat down at a Starbucks in Keller, TX to divide assets and discuss how to accomplish an amicable divorce. What started out as a 45-minute business meeting concluded after three hours of crying, praying, and embracing. When we sat down to talk, I had already decided: We were *through*. Our relationship was over. The chasm between us was too wide, and there was absolutely no way to cross it. But someone showed up in that coffee shop whom neither of us had expected – God. That afternoon, my wife's unconditional love, coupled with God's amazing grace, melted my heart of stone and saved our marriage.

It All Started with Coffee

Of course, that wasn't the first time we had a significant meeting at a coffee shop. Three and a half years earlier we met for a cup of joe shortly after connecting online. We were both very nervous. After all, we had each met a crazy person on the Internet and then agreed to meet for coffee! Our apprehension soon melted as we realized how easy it was to talk with one another. I loved her smile and the sparkle in her eyes. Tammy was drawn to my charisma and lack of "jerkiness" (believe me, it's totally a word).

After almost two hours of coffee and laughter, we were both getting hungry. We decided to continue our date across the street and have dinner together. We continued our enthralling conversation until they closed and kicked us out. Neither of us was ready for the evening to be over, so we drove to the DFW Airport observation area and talked for hours as planes flew overhead. I knew on that first night that we had something special. After a brief courtship, I proposed to Tammy and we got swept up in the momentum of new love, engagement, and glorious matrimony.

Life in the Blender

When we married on January 1, 2010, it wasn't the first rodeo for either one of us. Both of us had been married previously (me for almost ten years, Tammy for twelve) and we each brought three children into the marriage. Let that soak in for a minute – <u>six kids</u>!

Blending eight people into a cohesive family unit is no small task. Our families came from two different worlds. Tammy's crew enjoyed going out, while my herd was made of home-bodies. We had one TV in the house with no cable; Tammy's family had TVs in every room. My children were excellent communicators, but they couldn't cook food or do their own laundry to save their lives. Her kiddos were very self-sufficient, but extremely uncomfortable talking about their feelings. Oil, meet water.

In spite of our differences, the first year was pretty smooth. Memories were made. Parties were thrown. Vacations were taken. Everyone had so much fun together! Then reality set in. The newness wore off, my travel schedule intensified, and we found ourselves trying to balance work, church, a new marriage, the unique needs of six children, and the challenge of blending two very different families together. Our idyllic little Brady Bunch began to unravel.

The Fall

Looking back, I can clearly see how the stage was being set for failure. But at the time, I was oblivious to our slow fade toward marital collapse. Conflict between the kids. The stress of building a house. Moving for a third time in our short three-year marriage. Stress at work. Stress at home. Little priority placed on quality time, consistent date nights, sexual intimacy, shared activities, prayer together, romance, or any of the other elements that we would soon learn are essential for a successful marriage.

We could scarcely connect with those starry-eyed lovers who had met for coffee only a couple of years earlier. I rarely saw the sparkle that had once been so clear in Tammy's eyes. She rarely saw the charismatic gentlemen she had fallen in love with. Things were different now.

We tried everything we could think of to work through the conflict and ease the stress. Marriage counseling and family counseling. Marriage classes at church. A workshop on blended families. None of it worked. The kids continued to collide and our relationship limped along stubbornly. We were surviving, but it was a hollow victory.

In the midst of this turmoil and stress, I was naive to the dangers of a close friendship with a member of the opposite sex. Over a five-year period (longer than Tammy and I had even known each other), I had become very close with another woman. What began as an innocent friendship became a fatal virus that infected my mind and my marriage. As the stress at home and at work intensified, I turned to her for comfort and a sounding board. I even began to open up about frustrations that I was experiencing in my marriage, and she offered a sympathetic ear.

With my thread-bare marital bond and an intense work schedule, I drifted further and further from my first love (Jesus) and my second love (Tammy). In the fall of 2012, I began a two-month affair that threatened to destroy my soul, my wife, and my family. I became cold and distant. Overcome by guilt and shame, I didn't see any way out of the mess I had created, except to push for divorce. The thought of reconciliation seemed ridiculous to me. I still loved Tammy, but from my perspective there was simply no way she would ever accept me back. "If she knew what I had done," I thought, "she could never forgive me." Before giving us a chance to overcome, I had already assumed defeat in my own mind.

One day, while Tammy was headed out of town on a girl's trip, she asked me what was bothering me. I tried to blow it off, but she pressed me for details. Reluctantly, I dropped the bomb shell – "I'm not happy. I haven't been for a long time. I think we're over." Stunned, she got in the car and headed for the airport. For the next several days we talked. She cried. We fought. Rivers of tears flowed through Tammy's valley of despair. She knew that things weren't great, but she felt blind-sided by my desire for divorce. When she returned, we tried to work on the marriage, but the weight of my secret affair and the dual life I was living continued to poison my heart. After weeks of fighting and heartache, Tammy eventually gave in. Reluctantly, she and half the kiddos moved out of the house, and plans for divorce were in full swing by the end of the year.

Meanwhile, Tammy was devastated and perplexed. "How could things have spiraled out of control?" she wondered. "What caused him to change so quickly from the man I fell in love with, into this emotionless robot?" Something didn't add up.

Like a private eye, Tammy began to hunt and dig for answers. Facebook posts and song preferences. Behavioral changes and emotional changes. The pieces began to paint a frightening picture. Finally, a forgotten cell phone with undeleted text messages told enough of the story to confirm her suspicions.

The Showdown at Starbucks

At a coffee shop only minutes away from the first one where this relationship had begun, our lives and the lives of our six kiddos hung in the balance. As I began to discuss the division of assets, Tammy confronted me about the affair. Denying it at first, my walls eventually broke down as we talked more and cried more and struggled to dig through the remains of our once hopeful marriage. For three hours we poured out piles of emotion onto the tiny Starbucks table that sat between us (we can only imagine what the employees a few feet from us must have thought).

I walked into that coffee shop convinced our relationship had run its course. My devoted wife was not quite so ready to move on. Angry and bitter, she lashed out at me for my infidelity. She had every right to hate me, but through the tears I could hear love. As she spoke of her pain, I could hear hope. Grace walked hand in hand with her heartache.

"I'm not done loving you," she told me.

As we talked, her unconditional, Christ-like love shone through her anger and her tears. Three times I stopped her and asked: "Wait a minute, are you saying that you would actually be willing to work on saving our marriage, even after all I've put you through?" Each time, through her tears, she nodded "yes".

That meeting at Starbucks was difficult. But in the hurt, there was healing. Through grit, Tammy extended grace. And in the mangled mess we called a marriage, God began to work a miracle.

A New Proposal

The next day, I got down on one knee, just as I had three and a half years ago. I gave her a single rose and I asked her for the opportunity to prove to her that I was worth a second chance. "I don't know what the future holds," I told her. "I can't possibly predict the course of our healing process. I don't even know if it is possible. But if you will give me the chance, I will spend all of 2013 making it up to you. You don't have to commit to taking me back. I just need you to agree to give me a year to make things right."

She said yes.

Renewal

Rebuilding our relationship was both exciting and frightening, but we found few resources to guide us through the renewal process. We had to settle for books and conferences that focused on generic relationship topics such as emotional intimacy, communication, and prioritizing your relationship. Of course, these are crucial aspects to renewing your marriage. But none of it prepared us for the renewal process and the many emotional cycles of pain, fear, elation, doubt, joy, anger, ecstasy, peace, bitterness, and passion. While riding this emotional roller-coaster we had to continue investing time and energy reconstructing our friendship, rebuilding trust, and recognizing spiritual warfare and its impact on our marriage.

Throughout our renewal, God graciously provided us with mentors, scripture, books, marriage conferences, and online resources to put the broken pieces of our relationship together. As our bond grew, he began to send individuals and couples our way who were in similar situations. Long before we thought of having a formal ministry, we began pouring into other couples and sharing what was working, which furthered our own healing.

Our Phoenix Marriage

In Greek mythology, a phoenix is a bird which lives perpetually through a process of cyclical rebirth. According to legend, the death of one phoenix gives birth to another. At the end of its life, a phoenix ignites, engulfing itself in flames. Arising from those very same ashes, a new phoenix is born. The legend of the phoenix has been used for centuries as a symbol for rebirth, renewal, and change. It was even adopted by the early Christians to represent their rebirth through Christ.

For us, the phoenix symbolizes the birth of our new and improved, Christ-centered marriage. Tammy and I had a broken relationship that had crashed and burned to the ground. But like the mythological phoenix, our new marriage emerged from the ashes. From the remnants of our demolished marriage, God began a process of rebirth and renewal. He redeemed what had been lost. He revived what we thought had died.

God creates beauty out of ashes. He makes marriages out of messes. And He wants to work a miracle in yours.

Chapter One Reflections

1. What did you hear in our story that resonated with you?

2. In what ways have you allowed stress, life, work, or selfishness to get in the way of loving your spouse fully?

3. What has your spouse done, knowingly or unknowingly that has most severely wounded you?

4. How have you wounded your mate?

5. What, if anything, have you done to heal those wounds?

Commit to improving the openness in your marriage. Begin an honest discussion of how you have caused hurt and in turn been hurt in your marriage.

2

Marriages Eventually Get Messy

To be fully seen by somebody, then, and be loved anyhow - this is a human offering that can border on miraculous.

Elizabeth Gilbert,

Committed: A Skeptic Makes Peace with Marriage

B OY MEETS GIRL. *Girl notices boy is funny and charming. Boy notices girl is clever and free-spirited. Girl likes boy's sense of style. Boy likes how girl laughs at his jokes. Girl wonders how long she'll have to pretend to like his jokes.*

Girl and boy spend lots of time together and each feels butterflies in their stomachs when the other is around. Boy thinks about girl constantly. Girl thinks about boy constantly. Texts and notes fly furiously back and forth for weeks and months. Infatuation leads to courtship, courtship gives way to proposal, and finally the two "tie the knot" and begin an adventure known as marriage.

The boy and girl set out on this new chapter in life with energy and purpose. They know how "other" couples have let their relationships slip and their flame and passion fade. They are determined *not to fall into the same fate. Date night is a weekly event. Gifts and thoughtful expressions of love (a card, flower, favorite dessert, or sweet text message) are exchanged cheerfully and frequently. Affection they give freely and effortlessly as if there was no end to their passion for each other.*

Fast forward a few months or years, and the bliss has given way to the realities of life. There are jobs and bills and family dynamics to contend with. There are cars and schedules and a house to manage. In time, children may arrive, bringing blessings, challenges, and ultimately, more stress.

In the midst of all the chaos, entrenched patterns set in. Patterns for time spent, words exchanged, and effort exerted. Date nights slip from a weekly event to a monthly or bi-monthly event. Gifts are exchanged at appointed times as dictated by the calendar. And the raw and passionate affection is cheaply traded for a hollow, tired, and rehearsed exchange.

You know the story too well. You've seen it played out a thousand times in the lives of your parents, your siblings, your friends, and perhaps even your own marriage. But this is the natural course of a relationship, right? Eventually you have to grow up, quit dreaming, and accept that marriage is more about life-long commitment than life-enriching companionship. Can this be all there is for marriage?

God wants more for your marriage

God wants more for your marriage than just surviving. He wants more than roommates pooling their assets. He has a grand plan for what you can do together as a team. Each of you brings unique talents, abilities, background, and experiences to produce a powerful combination.

"It is not good for the man to be alone." – Gen 2:18

"My God will meet all your needs according to the riches of His glory in Christ Jesus." – Phil 4:19

"He who finds a wife finds what is good and receives favor from the LORD." – Proverbs 18:22

"For I know the plans I have for you," declares the LORD, "plans to prosper you and not to harm you, plans to give you hope and a future." – Jeremiah 29:11

In other words:

1) Being alone is a bad thing. We were designed as relational beings.

2) God will supply our needs, including our need to not be alone.

3) Finding a spouse is a blessing.

4) God has huge plans for you and a future full of hope.

Nowhere in those passages (or anywhere else in scripture) does God say we are to settle for a reluctant roommate or a cold co-existence. God desires so much more for you.

- He establishes the **plan** in Genesis (<u>leave</u> your family of origin and <u>cleave</u> to your spouse).

- He describes the **promise** throughout Proverbs (if you seek wisdom, reject folly, cling to what is good, reject what is evil, cherish and protect your relationships, then you will have peace).

- The fruits of **passion** spring out of a healthy relationship, as described in Song of Solomon (fiery passion doesn't just die on its own; we stop feeding the fire and it naturally goes out).

- The **pattern** for success is illustrated in I Corinthians 13 (Love believes all things, Love hopes all things, Love never fails).

That's great, but my marriage is hopeless

Sadly, many couples have lost hope of the bright future God desires for their marriage. While their marriage may not be completely dead, it is rotten with the stench of death hanging in air. Entrenched in the past and overwhelmed with the present the couple has lost the will to push through the pain and problems that plague them. Yet where there is darkness, the Bible offers light. Where there is exhaustion, Jesus offers refreshment.

Does God really work that way? Is there really hope?

- God **gives** courage. *He led Gideon's 300 men to defeat over 100,000 Midianites.*

- God **changes** hearts. *Saul became Paul, transforming from a persecutor of Christians to a preacher of converts.*

- God **restores** hope. *For a lost and dying world, He restored hope by delivering his son as the ultimate sacrifice.*

If God specializes in giving, changing, and restoring, then why are so many Christian marriages in distress? It's quite simple.

We live in a fallen, dysfunctional world which threatens your marriage:

- Boredom

- Pain

- Disappointment

- Infidelity

- Distractions

- Anger

- Fear

- Depression

- Apathy

- Resentment

- Porn

- Bitterness

- Stress

But none of that matters because you have Jesus on your side. He conquered sin and death because of His love for you. None of that matters because you and your spouse are children of the King. He desires a full life for you and your family, and no relationship is so broken that it can't be pieced back together in the name of Jesus (Philippians 4:13). Our God is a God of second chances. He's the God of underdogs. He specializes in renewal. It is impossible for you to mess up your marriage so badly that He can't fix it. Time, sweat, tears, and lots of prayer can restore *any* relationship.

I don't even know where to begin

Whether you are just beginning to recognize the erosion of your marriage or your marriage has already crumbled; don't fret. You can prevail. My wife and I have been through the wringer, and we have had the privilege of walking with other couples who have suffered the devastation of complacency, heartache, dishonesty, infidelity, anger, bitterness, and resentment. We have made it, and so can you. You may not be able to see it right now, but **there is still hope**.

- Section I: "Up In Flames" – How marriages drift, fall apart, crumble, dissolve, and burst into flames.

- Section II: "Rebuild, Renew, and Restore" – Building your marriage God's way.

- Section III: "Beauty out of Ashes" – Enjoying and protecting the gift of your renewed relationship.

The Power of Testimony

My wife and I have an incredibly loving and happy relationship. We are truly each other's soulmate. But our relationship hasn't always been so cheerful and the future hasn't always looked so bright. Throughout the book, we will share insight into our marriage and renewal journey.

In addition to sharing our story, a handful of couples have agreed to share their own experiences from walking through the process of renewal. You'll find those encouraging messages in Appendix B – Testimonies of Marriage Renewal. Through our own journey and others we have walked alongside, we have come to accept that **no heart is too hard and no marriage is so broken that God can't redeem it. Give him your mess, and he'll work a miracle.**

God is in the business of fresh starts, second chances, and renewal. You and your spouse owe it to yourselves to give your marriage another chance. Give God the opportunity to show up and transform your hearts as he has been doing for thousands of years. The final chapter in your love story is yet to be written.

Chapter Two Reflections

1. God wants more for your marriage. He has a **plan** and a **promise**. He desires **passion** following a **pattern** of love.

    a. Which of these is easy for you to believe?

    b. Which is harder for you to accept?

2. What has threatened your marriage now or in the past?

- Boredom
- Pain
- Disappointment
- Infidelity
- Distractions
- Anger
- Fear
- Depression
- Apathy
- Resentment
- Porn
- Bitterness
- Stress

Often couples experiencing difficulty feel isolated and hopeless. Testimony is powerful. You'll find stories of hope in **Appendix B – Testimonies of Marriage Renewal**.

Section I

Up in Flames

How marriages drift, fall apart, crumble, dissolve, and burst into flames

3

The Natural Arc of a Relationship

The course of true love never did run smooth.

William Shakespeare
A Midsummer Night's Dream

Love does not appear with any warning signs. You fall into it as if pushed from a high diving board. No time to think about what's happening. It's inevitable. An event you can't control. A crazy, heart-stopping, roller-coaster ride that just has to take its course.

Jackie Collins
Lucky

I REMEMBER MY FIRST ENCOUNTER with romantic love, like it was yesterday. We met in school. She was attracted to my clever sense of humor. I was entranced by her radiant smile and her beautiful eyes. We passed notes in class, ate lunch together every day, and spent time together every chance we could. It was a magical relationship, until she broke my heart. One day I was attributing every love song on the radio to our relationship and imagining our future, and the next day I was a broken-hearted puddle of tears. I was a mess. I put the "hopeless" in "hopeless romantic." I pined for weeks, cried at nearly every song that came on the radio and acted like a fool. Of course, I was only in first grade.

Over the years I learned to cope with a broken heart a bit more gracefully, but I learned early how fickle romantic love can be. More importantly, I learned that as my capacity for romantic love grew with age, so too did my capacity for experiencing pain when my heart repeatedly broke.

Lunatics and Love Birds

Falling in love is exhilarating. It consumes your thoughts, your emotions, your energy, your soul, and your sanity. It drives you wild with anticipation and delights your senses with visions of the future. Lunatics and love birds share a great deal in common. The main difference is that lunatics don't tend to frequent flower shops.

At some point, the frenzy of new love fades and the relationship routine ensues. Relationships follow a rather natural pattern. They begin with mutual enjoyment and fulfillment (relationships would never begin if this weren't true). As patterns set in and routines emerge, a predictable plateau is experienced. Initially, that plateau is pleasant and comforting. Over time, some become disenchanted due to what they perceive as a loss in momentum. Sooner or later a crisis occurs, typically when much of the bloom is off of the proverbial rose. That crisis might be dramatic and spectacular or it may merely be a slow fade into monotony. Eventually, the relationship eases into a maintenance mode. There are some highs and some lows, but overall the relationship slides into a comfortable and predictable pattern and a dangerous slope of apathy.

The Rise and Fall of Love

"He fell in love."

"She fell out of love."

The verb *fall* implies lack of control. We get swept up in the emotional momentum and allow it to carry us away.

Being driven by emotion is exhilarating and intoxicating on the up-swing, but when the frenzy fades and the emotional energy dissipates, we have to find a way to survive. We cope with long hours at work, going out with friends, and weekends of golf or hunting. We cope with shopping, volunteering at school, or getting involved at church. After all, this is what adults do. This is how relationships are supposed to evolve. *Right?*

In fact, it's *better* this way (we tell ourselves). Love requires a lot of work and energy, and who has piles of that lying around? All that kissing and hugging and being-excited-to-see-each-other is exhausting. Just think of how much time you can save now that you aren't writing notes, and sending text messages! You'll be able to get so much more accomplished. And what about all the money you've been throwing away on flowers and dinners and gifts! If you'd only fallen out of love sooner you'd have even *more money* and *more time* to get things done!

At some point we accept that the passion and energy we initially felt must be exchanged for a more comfortable, familiar, predictable version of our relationship. This is the natural order of things. Doesn't Ecclesiastes say: "There is a time for everything, and a season for every activity under the heavens?" Then there must be a time to fall in love and a time to fall out of love.

But for some reason, you are not at peace. Something within you cries out for more. Something in you yearns for the dizzying heights of love that you once felt. You yearn for the excitement; you ache for the passion; your soul longs for the overwhelming emotional tsunami to overtake you again.

But it doesn't.

You don't get magically swept up in a tidal wave of puppy love. Your heart does not ooze with passion. Cupid does not impale you or your spouse. The two of you are left in a bit of a daze, wondering where to go from here.

The Apathy Cycle

Where did the flame go? How did the passion die? Was it all just a phase? Is every relationship doomed to deflate, leaving the once starry-eyed lovers seeking solace in their own hobbies / work / friends / projects / distractions?

Grappling with the loss of that emotional intensity can be difficult. There's a considerable feeling of emptiness and disillusionment. From this point, one or both spouses tend to get caught in the "apathy cycle," consisting of five phases that tend to repeat: *disillusionment, mourning, bitterness, coping, re-energizing,* and *fatigue.*

- **Disillusionment phase**: One or both lovers become disillusioned with the idea of love and romance. They exchange passion and spontaneity for prescriptive and comfortable routines. They may resort to a more formal, ritualistic approach to the relationship, driven by patterns of expectation and formulaic overtures – flowers on Valentine's Day, fancy anniversary dinner, monthly date night (dinner and a movie), Mother's / Father's Day, etc. Some couples can remain in this phase indefinitely, but they always run the risk of slipping into the mourning phase.

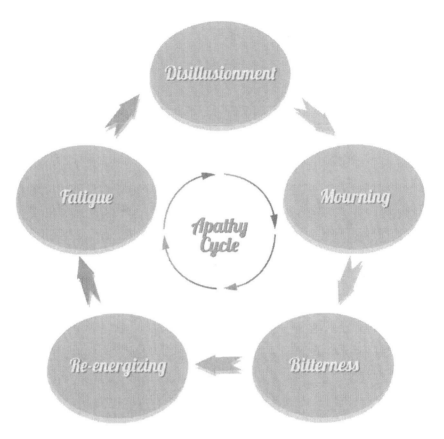

- **Mourning phase**: This phase is characterized by mourning the loss of what the relationship once was and wondering where and when things went so wrong. Discouragement, detachment, and distraction are all common side effects of this phase. On occasion one or both partners may lift themselves out of the mourning phase, alternately their mourning may give way to the next phase – bitterness.

- **Bitterness phase**: On the downward side of the cycle, one or both spouses may slide into bitterness, resentment, or even anger. Fuses are short, squabbles occur, and the distance between the couple grows – he forgets to take out the trash and it's evidence he doesn't love her; she neglects to call while on a business trip and it's proof she doesn't care. Left unchecked, the bitterness phase leads to anger, separation or divorce, and even affairs (emotional and physical).

- **Coping phase**: Humans are highly adaptive creatures by nature. In this phase, the couple adopts coping mechanisms to occupy their time, their thoughts, and to distract them away from the pain and frustration that exists within the marriage.

- **Re-energizing phase**: Whether by chance, the cycles of the moon, or sheer force of will, relationships improve. The couple begins to experience a brief taste of the joy and elation that they once felt. Dates are fun, conversations are interesting, and for a little while, things seem to be heading in the right direction.

- **Fatigue phase**: The effort and energy expended during the re-energizing phase often dissipate, plunging the relationship back into a fresh cycle of disillusionment and mourning.

The apathy cycle plagues so many couples. After descending from the early emotional highs and settling into a cycle of good and bad phases, couples often become complacent. They accept this as just the natural course of things. They stop trying to achieve the levels of joy and fulfillment they once had, accepting this cheaper substitute of good and bad seasons in its place.

Round and round the cycle goes, week after week and month after month. With each iteration, the couple becomes further resigned to their plight as the perpetual wheel of apathy wears on their collective patience.

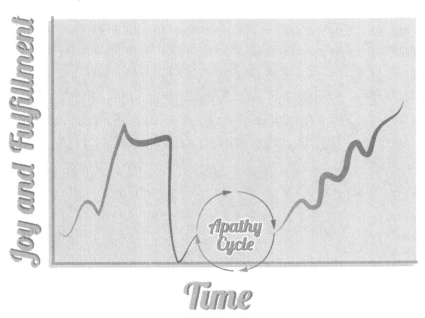

> **Our marriage** – The apathy cycle is an emotionally draining routine with which Tammy and I are all too familiar. Each of us having been married for 9+ years prior, we experienced how it robs a couple of joy and rips the bonds holding you together. What we weren't prepared for, however, is that awareness of the problem isn't sufficient to solve it. If you don't build your marriage on a solid, Christ-centered footing, you can still get caught in the apathy cycle even if you know to look for it. Two Christians getting married does not a Christ-centered marriage make. Daily prayer, dying to self, and serving each other does.

Somewhere Out There...

Remember my first girlfriend? She was really something special. Erin...something, I'm not really sure what her last name was, but she was a cutie pie. I really think we could have had a future together. But her dad got transferred, they moved to another state, and I was left to pick up the shattered pieces of my heart. I pined for weeks and teared up every time I heard the theme song from "An American Tail" (1986).

> *Somewhere out there*
>
> *Beneath the pale moonlight*
>
> *Someone's thinking of me*
>
> *And loving me tonight*
>
> *Somewhere out there*
>
> *Someone's saying a prayer*
>
> *That we'll find one another*
>
> *In that big somewhere out there...*

You and your soulmate have *already found each other* in that "big somewhere out there." You may be a bit more banged up and bruised than when you first met. You're likely tired and less enthusiastic about your future. But this isn't the final chapter of this book and it's not the final chapter of your lives together. The apathy cycle **can** be broken. It is possible for you and your mate to rebirth your marriage into something fresh, new, and deeply fulfilling.

Chapter Three Reflections

1. What phase(s) of the apathy cycle do you recognize in your own marriage?

- Disillusionment

- Mourning

- Bitterness

- Coping

- Re-energizing

- Fatigue

2. Which phase do you and your spouse tend to get stuck in most often?

3. How has the apathy cycle robbed your marriage of joy?

4

Spiritual Warfare

Be alert and of sober mind. Your enemy, the devil, prowls around like a roaring lion looking for someone to devour.

I Peter 5:8

There is no neutral ground in the universe; every square inch, every split second is claimed by God and counterclaimed by Satan.

C.S. Lewis
"Christianity and Culture," Christian Reflections

H E FORGETS TO TAKE OUT THE TRASH *for the 3rd time this month. Is he forgetful or does he just not care?*

She comes home late from the office AGAIN. Maybe she's busy with an important project, or maybe she's a selfish workaholic, content to leave you with all the responsibilities to care for the kids and the house.

Work, play, responsibilities, kid's activities, finances, sexual intimacy, vacations, and holidays are all fertile ground for conflict. You pack your days and weeks full of commitments and activities, creating stress and pressure. The stress escalates and your emotions inevitably spill over onto your mate. And as you experience such challenges, there is always the opportunity to see these obstacles in the best possible light or to steer the situation toward negativity.

Remember the devil and angel that would appear on the shoulders of cartoon characters? In a very real sense, there is a constant battle for your mind. Hidden amongst the trivial, common activities filling your day is a battlefield in which the enemy is posturing, plotting, and scheming. The longer you can stay in the "apathy cycle," the more seeds of doubt, fear, bitterness, anger, resentment, and selfishness are planted. Little by little, the enemy is seeking to gain ground and drive a wedge between you and your spouse.

We are at war

Spiritual warfare is not a myth. It's not a game and it's not a theory. It is a real and present danger for every believer, not just the ones on the "front lines" in active ministry. In the movie, *The Usual Suspects*, Kevin Spacey says: "The greatest trick the Devil ever pulled – was convincing the world he didn't exist."

If the enemy can convince you that reality is something you only experience through your five senses, then he has successfully detached you from the most important truth –

you are a spiritual being and the decisions you make have spiritual consequences. Detaching you in this way is a dangerous mindset, because the more important and 'real' your physical life becomes, the easier it is to get trapped into the perpetual, destructive "apathy cycle".

But hold on! We're talking about marriage, not church. I mean, sure, Satan cares about attacking missionaries and thwarting conversions, and tempting us to make mistakes and get tripped up by sin, but he doesn't care about my marriage...does he?

Try, for a moment, to step into the enemy's shoes (I believe they are made by Prada). If you were going to craft a cunning master plan for destroying the church, which strategy would you predict to be more successful?

- **Strategy A – Frontal Assault:** Attack people actively engaged in ministry. Tempt people to sin during worship, distract passionate believers from their respective callings, and block evangelistic efforts. Anywhere that the kingdom is advancing, you apply your resources in an attempt to counter such progress.

- **Strategy B – Dissolve from Within:** The church is made up of people and people are held together through close-knit family bonds. Attack these relationships, erode their bonds, and create division wherever possible. If the family is sufficiently distracted and distressed, then there can be no genuine movement of God's people.

To be sure, the enemy likely uses a mix of the two strategies, but the second approach is clearly the smarter angle. A *frontal assault* is easy to recognize and those involved are primed for a fight. These are people on the front lines of kingdom work, and they are actively preparing their minds and hearts for combat. The *dissolution from within* strategy is more subtle, more distressing, and ultimately more crippling.

The enemy wants your marriage to fail

Nothing could make Satan happier than to see your marriage crash and burn. As the flames engulf your union, pieces of your life and people connected to you will also catch fire until you, your spouse, your children, and those you love are sucked into the pain and bitterness of a failed relationship. In the HBO series *Game of Thrones*, a particularly devilish character has an unquenchable thirst for power with no bounds:

"He would see this country burn if he could be king of the ashes."

Let's re-imagine that sentence in the context of spiritual warfare and your marriage: "<u>The Devil</u> would see <u>your marriage</u> burn, if he could be king of the ashes."

And so he *plots* and *schemes* and *suggests* and *insinuates* and *reminds* and *agitates* and *abrasively erodes* any spiritual fruit in your heart. Consider his strategy.

How to dissolve a marriage

- Focus on how your spouse isn't meeting your needs

- Revisit times when your spouse has hurt you

- Wait for your spouse to make the first move in apologizing, diffusing, or resolving conflict

- Dwell on your spouse's faults and short-comings

- Allow the fear of getting hurt again (just like your spouse hurt you last week or last month) overwhelm you and steal your peace of mind

- Take a defensive posture to protect yourself from potential pain

- When your spouse hurts your feelings, stuff them deep down rather than voicing them and working together to solve the problem

- Play games, nag, manipulate, to have your needs met first

- Prioritize your own activities and interests over spending time with your spouse

- Blame your spouse for your eroding relationship rather than taking responsibility for your own laziness and self-centeredness

This clever approach has been used for centuries. The tools of pain, bitterness, resentment, anger, fear, and apathy are the enemy's specialty. With these tools, the devil saps your energy, chips away at your patience, whittles away your resolve, and breaks down your commitment to be selfless. Over time, a widening gap emerges.

<u>Your spiritual bond dissolves first</u>. It starts innocently enough. Carving out time in the day for Bible study is hard and the Bible sometimes seems so detached from modern life anyway. With all of the kid's activities, there never seems to be an available weekend to do a ministry project together. And although praying together sounds like a good idea, it feels so uncomfortable and awkward.

Next, the enemy moves in:

Remember how she was neglecting you earlier today? And now she wants to pray? Does she think everything is just magically better?

Of course it would be great to study the Bible together, but she won't want to do that with you after lost your temper with her earlier. You have absolutely no ground to stand on today.

Next, your emotional connection follows. The stress of life, kids, and work wears on you both. You don't have the emotional energy to pour into notes and gifts and 'just thinking of you' text messages throughout the day. You can't remember the last time that you had a real date night together (apart from the obligatory Anniversary or Valentine's Day). In the midst of this fading emotional connection, the enemy begins to sow seeds of dissent once again:

You've had a hard day, would it kill him to show a little tenderness and compassion?

Why does she always have to bring things back around to money? Doesn't she care about anything else?

With your spiritual and emotional union on life support, your physical chemistry doesn't stand a chance. Despite Hollywood's imagery, physical chemistry is not something that spontaneously happens when two attractive people enter a room. If you make yourself emotionally vulnerable to another human being and invest quality time with him or her, physical chemistry is likely to follow. If you add spiritual intimacy to the equation, the physical chemistry is guaranteed. The corollary is also true. Remove emotional and spiritual intimacy from the equation, and your physical intimacy is sure to follow.

Predictably, the enemy is not blind to your fading intimacy. Instead, he pounces on the opportunity to driver a deeper wedge between you two (I Peter 5:8). He continues his barrage of lies, casting blame and planting doubts and insinuations:

Why should you put forth the effort to be romantic? All she ever does is nag you.

He'd probably rather spend time with his buddies than take you out on a date. It's no wonder you don't feel passionate and excited about seeing him at the end of the day.

All of this creeps up over time. Satan is patient. Very patient. He'll plan the demise of your union for months and even years. In *The Screwtape Letters*, C.S. Lewis portrays a picture of how the enemy might plot and scheme to detach us from our true callings. In one letter, the older demon passes the following advice to his young apprentice:

"Indeed the safest road to Hell is the gradual one – the gentle slope, soft underfoot, without sudden turnings, without milestones, without signposts."

And so it goes with our marriages.

> **Our marriage** – We have come to recognize spiritual warfare – that battlefield which takes place in your mind – quite readily. But during our first three years of marriage, we were unaware. We allowed the enemy to plant selfishness and bitterness, and we then nurtured these feelings into resentment. I felt the sting of neglect and Tammy felt the pressure of not measuring up to my expectations. The deep-seeded, persistent negative feelings we felt for each other were manufactured so subtly that they felt natural and justified. The clever lies always do.

Portrait of a Broken Marriage

Legal divorce isn't the only indication of a broken marriage. While every relationship goes through seasons, there are different degrees of detachment and isolation (resulting from the erosion of your spiritual, emotional, and physical bonds) that constitute a broken relationship. Such travesties come in a variety of shapes and sizes. Consider the following portraits of broken marriages:

- **Busy bees** – *Date nights are few and far between. Tokens of love are rarely exchanged.*

Joint prayer and Bible study is sporadic and almost always in response to a crisis. Conversations center on schedules, work, and finances rather than your mission, your passion, and your future together. It's as if the spark of life has been removed from your relationship.

The enemy doesn't have to completely destroy your marriage to win. All he needs to do is distract you with schedules, activities, and stress. Amidst this hectic rhythm, a general malaise overcomes your relationship and you both miss out on the joy and fulfillment God intends for you as a couple.

- **Roommates** – *Date nights happen infrequently, typically spurred by the calendar (anniversary, Valentine's Day, and birthday). Conversations are short and to the point. Neither of you goes out of your way to spend time with one another. You each have your own hobbies and your own friends. You share a roof, but not your thoughts. You share a checkbook, but not your emotions. You share a family, but not your passion or dreams. You may be physically in the same room, but your hearts are miles apart from each other. Living parallel lives in isolation, your spirits whither and fade.*

Some couples settle into a shared living arrangement, devoid of tenderness or emotional intimacy. Each spouse lives their own life apart from sharing assets, meals, and holidays. It's a hollow existence that robs the couple of joy, peace, and genuine companionship.

- **Affair** – *It starts out innocently enough. Friendly banter, shared interests, interesting conversations, and time spent together through a project at work, or as a workout partner at the gym. This level of familiarity is dangerous and sets the stage for deeper levels of emotional intimacy. Eventually you let your defenses down and begin to confide in one another. Once the topic turns to discussing problems at home, it's a slippery slope toward moral failure.*

There is not a more selfish or toxic season in a marriage than an affair. Whether purely emotional or also physical, an affair strikes at the core of any relationship. You may think you're immune, but don't be naive. *Under the right circumstances, **anyone** can succumb to an affair.* Affairs don't start spontaneously. They begin because the couple has stopped investing in their marriage. Apathy creates distance, leading to loneliness and a widening gap in the relationship. It is the space within that gap that creates a ripe environment for one or both partners to make a life-altering, selfish decision. Satan has paved this road to infidelity for countless couples and he'll jump at the opportunity to trap you in the same spiral of shame and guilt.

- **Separation or Divorce** – The sentiments are all too common:

"Sometimes these things just happen."

"We're just different people."

"We want different things in life."

"We used to be in love, but not anymore."

"We should have never gotten married."

The ultimate evidence of a broken marriage is separation or divorce. Sadly, for far too many couples, the dissolution of their divine union had begun long before attorneys got involved. Divorce is destructive, poisonous, and has long lasting consequences, sometimes for generations. It's no wonder that God hates divorce (Malachi 2:16).

Is it too late?

Repairing a broken marriage isn't easy. No matter where you are in the healing process, putting the broken pieces back together requires a tremendous amount of effort. The more pain the two of you have experienced, the harder it will be to overcome the past and rebuild the trust, **but it can be done**.

Wherever you might be, the enemy has worked hard to isolate you. You are isolated from each other, and isolated from the source of peace – your Heavenly Father. You and your mate are starving for attention, affection, warmth, and comfort. **The tragedy, is you are probably reading this book right next to the very person that God has _chosen_ to serve as the physical extension of His love for you.** Through the mind, body, and soul of your mate, God wants to reach out and connect with you in an authentic and holy way. So take heart, keep reading, and prepare to embark upon a difficult, but valuable journey to harmony and mutual fulfillment.

Chapter Four Reflections

1. Revisit the list on page 46, "How to dissolve a marriage." Can you relate to one or more of those toxic scenarios? If so, how have they impacted your marriage?

2. On 1 to 10 scale (10 being the highest), rate the following qualities of your marriage over the last <u>three months</u>:

- Spiritual bond

- Emotional connection

- Physical chemistry

3. Fill in the blanks:

- The greatest trick the devil ever pulled was

  _____

- The safest road to Hell is the _____ one

- Wherever you might be, the enemy has worked hard to _____ you

- You and your mate are both starving for

  _____, _____, _____, _____

5

Myths About Healing Relationships

What seems to us as bitter trials are often blessings in disguise.

Oscar Wilde

Eventually you will come to understand that love heals everything, and love is all there is.

Gary Zukav

T HE "DEVIL'S BACKBONE" was a long stretch of untended woods that backed up to the neighborhood where I grew up in Euless, TX. It seemed that every kid had a spooky story connected to Devil's Backbone. Lost pets, inexplicable lights and noises, and paranormal activity were all rumored to be the work of those forbidden woods. Tales of axe murders and occult rituals were shared in hushed tones for fear that someone might be listening. It wasn't until I was older that I first heard the term "urban myth," but I knew instantly that the mystique surrounding the Devil's Backbone fit the bill. A few years ago, I went back for a visit to my old neighborhood. Despite the hype I remember as a kid, I found an unassuming collection of trees, overgrown vines, and beer cans. Myth busted.

We are all guilty, at some level, of believing myths previous generations have handed down and our own minds have perpetuated. Through stories, conversations, and convenient anecdotes, we reinforce half-truths.

<u>Commonly believed myths</u>

- You can get a cold...from being cold (ummm...no, colds are more common when it's cold because people stay inside, breathe the same air and touch things).

- Carrots improve your eye sight (WWII propaganda aimed at convincing the Axis that vegetables, not technology, was the secret to our pilots aerial prowess).

- Bananas grow on trees (nope, it's a plant).

- If you cut an earthworm in half, you'll get two earthworms (not true, one half regenerates and the other half dies).

There comes a time when we have to take stock of the myths that we have bought into for years. In the case of relationship myths, that time is <u>now</u>.

The Myth of Repetition

Human beings have a remarkable capacity for change. And yet, all too often when it comes to healing a broken relationship, we seem to buy the argument that people are incapable of turning over a new leaf.

- *She can't change. She'll always act that way.*

- *Old habits die hard.*

- *He's just too stubborn. There's no way he would be willing to change.*

- *You can't teach an old dog new tricks.*

- *Once a cheat, always a cheat.*

As common as these thoughts are, they simply aren't true. Just because you have done something before doesn't necessarily mean you will do it again. Likewise, a pattern of behavior can be changed. You can learn to express your love in a language[1] your spouse understands.

> **Our marriage** – The myth of repetition played a significant part in the downfall of our marriage. I was convinced that Tammy couldn't change patterns of thought and behavior that were damaging our bond.

---

[1] Gary Chapman (1995). The Five Love Languages: How to Express Heartfelt Commitment to Your Mate.

One of the areas where we wrestled with this was in the realm of our love languages. My number one love language is physical affection. I give enormous bear hugs, hand out back scratches like candy, and would rather go without food than go without affection. I love to kiss, hug, and snuggle. Tammy, on the other hand, is not naturally affectionate. She is more reserved in physical expressions of love and often forgets to communicate through touch. This disparity between my primary love language of affection and her primary love language of quality time led to resentment. After more than three years of marriage and multiple attempts to communicate how vital physical touch was for me, hopelessness set in. I feared that Tammy was incapable of changing and that I would be doomed to remain in a cold, unloving void.

No matter how habitual a behavior might be, genuine change is possible. Consider the following examples from the Bible:

- Saul, the persecutor of Christians was transformed into Paul, the preacher of converts.

- Peter, who denied Christ three times, was changed into one of the boldest leaders in the early church.

- Rahab a prostitute in the Old Testament demonstrated such faith in God that she is mentioned in the 'honor roll of faith' in the thirteenth chapter of Hebrews.

Scripture is filled with these kinds of transformations. When someone encounters God authentically and truly surrenders themselves, there is no limit to the change of heart, attitude, and temperament they can experience. As Jesus said, "With God, all things are possible." (Matthew 19:26).

The Myth of Severity

So change is possible, but unfortunately, it often feels as if it is too late. There's simply no way to overcome the depth and breadth of damage that has occurred. Or at least, that's what Satan would have you believe.

It's a lie.

The pain in your relationship is severe, but God's grace and healing is far more powerful. The myth of severity can take a couple of different forms:

- *It's too late; our relationship is too far gone to be restored.*

- *I've already been hurt so much; I don't want to get hurt again.*

- *I can't forgive her for what she's done to me.*

- *I can't forgive myself for what I've done to her.*

The myth of severity magnifies two crippling emotions: *fear* and *guilt*. You fear that if you continue in the marriage, one or both of you will just get hurt more. Any potential progress is thwarted. Fear prevents the one who is hurt from taking the risk, and it paralyzes the offending party for fear that they will make things worse.

The looming weight of guilt from months – or years – of damage hangs heavy on your hearts and souls. You have both made mistakes, and the guilt of those mistakes makes you feel worthless and ill-equipped to face the challenge of restoring your withering bond. Fortunately, combating fear and absolving guilt is God's specialty.

Our marriage – This myth hit us at two different times. First, I bought into it in a big way during my affair. There were multiple points in those months where I considered confessing to Tammy in an effort to reconcile.

But each time, I became overwhelmed with guilt and fear. I had gone too far. I had violated her trust and there was simply no way she could possibly take me back once she knew. I gave up before we even had a chance to save our marriage. The second time this myth trapped us was once we decided that we wanted to work on our marriage. We still had significant hurdles to overcome in order to renew our tattered relationship. The severity of damage seemed insurmountable. Bitterness and resentment had been building for years, coupled with substantial heartbreak and violations of trust from my affair. Throughout our renewal process we feared that the pain we had experienced and the guilt that I carried was simply too great to overcome. This myth nearly wrecked our renewal.

Though the severity of pain in your marriage may seem overwhelming, you have a great physician in your corner. Jesus is a compassionate healer:

- Jesus is sympathetic and compassionate towards our weaknesses (Hebrews 4:15-16).

- His perfect love casts out fear (I John 4:18).

- If he can calm a storm, he can calm your hearts (Mark 4:35-39).

- Jesus has compassion for prodigals (Luke 15:11-32).

- He delivers freedom and healing to the broken-hearted (Luke 4:18, Matthew 5:4, Psalm 34:18, Psalm 147:3).

A mountain of pain might stand between you and your spouse, but Jesus has the power to move mountains.

The Myth of Fatalism

When you see something happen often enough, you come to believe it will always work out that way. If you see a flawed relationship model repetitively demonstrated, you develop a warped perception of marriage. More importantly, it builds an expectation that there isn't another possibility. It may seem as though some – or even ALL – relationships are doomed.

- *This is just what happens. Eventually all marriages devolve into a shadow of what they once were.*

- *Some relationships just weren't meant to be. It's better to start over with someone else and hope things work out better this time.*

- *My sister/cousin/neighbor/friend said that my marriage is hopeless, so I should take their advice, give up and move on.*

No relationship is doomed. No matter how dire the situation may seem, God is capable of breathing new life into any marriage. All you need is two willing people, plus lots of prayer and hard work. In fact, we have seen situations where one partner's prayer and persistence changes the heart of the unwilling spouse to make reconciliation possible.

The "I Can't" Myth

Ever since we were children, we have relied upon a cowardly excuse – I just **can't**. Why can't you? You can't because you don't know how. You can't because it's too hard. You can't because you're unsure it will work. The fear of failure looms over you, taunting you, and paralyzing you. Of course, we dress up this excuse more than we did when we were children. Do any of these sound familiar?

- *I don't know how to fix things. I don't even know where to start!*

- *We've been locked into our routines for so many years; I don't see how we can possibly change.*

- *We don't have strong communication skills. If we can't talk, how can we possibly rebuild our bond?*

> **Our marriage** – In the year and a half leading up to the near-collapse of our marriage we encountered periods of discouragement. Hopelessness and doubt overwhelmed us as we focused upon our challenges and why things wouldn't work. At times, each of us was plagued with negativity. Unable and unwilling to see the vision of what our marriage could become, we resigned ourselves to marital apathy. Having each come from previous failed marriages, it was easy for us to give up and assume defeat.

Using the "I can't" excuse has been a strategy for thousands of years. Moses even tried it in Exodus 3 and 4. God called Moses to lead the children of Israel out of Egypt. Moses' response to God:

- He wasn't worthy (3:11)

- He wouldn't know what to tell people (3:13)

- The people wouldn't believe him (4:1)

- He wasn't eloquent enough (4:10)

With each excuse, God told Moses to trust and obey. God continued to reassure him this was all part of His plan. Furthermore, God promised to provide Moses with the words and the courage needed to be successful. Do you think that He will do any less for your marriage? Remember, that God has great plans for you and your mate (Jeremiah 29:11). Your marriage has a purpose in the kingdom and God will meet you more than half-way if you are willing to put in the work.

Can my marriage really be restored?

Relationships and human emotions are surprisingly resilient. God has made us to be incredibly adaptive creatures, able to cope, heal, and ultimately, to overcome. Additionally, as believers, we have the ability to tap into God's immeasurable grace and power. Through the Holy Spirit, we can learn how to obtain peace and overcome even the most bitter obstacles standing between us and our mate.

Removing your mental block is a critical aspect of healing. Your relationship might appear to be irreparably broken. The gulf between you may seem too great. But this mindset is preventing you from experiencing the simple truths of grace, forgiveness, and healing. Other couples have experienced similar pain and successfully managed to knit their relationships back together. More importantly, they rebuild their bonds stronger and healthier than they were before. Put your mental blocks and excuses to rest, setting the stage for healing.

Being cold won't cause you to catch a cold. Eating carrots won't dramatically improve your eyesight. Earthworms don't multiply when you cut them. And you don't have to accept the common myths that negative people perpetuate. With God on your side, you can overcome the myths of repetition and severity. You can reject the lie of fatalism. And you can put to rest the "I can't" excuses.

Reject the myths and embrace the truth. Like so many other marriages before you, your marriage can be renewed, restored, and rebuilt, stronger than it has ever been.

Chapter Five Reflections

1. The **Myth of Repetition** claims that you and your spouse can't change your ways. Has this myth played a part in your relationship?

2. The **Myth of Severity** purports that once enough damage has been done, there is no way to save your marriage. Has this taken hold in your marriage?

3. Simply because something has occurred before is no guarantee it will happen again. Yet, the **Myth of Fatalism** would have you believe all marriages are doomed to fail. Have either of you wrestled with this myth?

4. The **"I Can't" Myth** can be paralyzing. If you don't know how to fix your relationship, it's hard to make things better. Can you relate to this myth?

Section II

Rebuild, Renew, and Restore

Building your marriage God's way

6

Lay the Foundation

There is only one secure foundation: a genuine, deep relationship with Jesus Christ, which will carry you through any and all turmoil. No matter what storms are raging all around, you'll stand firm if you stand on His love.

Charles Stanley

T HE STRONGEST SIMPLE GEOMETRIC SHAPE is the triangle. Weight is evenly and efficiently distributed to preserve the structural integrity. To create stronger shapes, you simply utilize combinations of triangles. Bridges, which must support thousands of pounds of weight are made possible by tresses, comprised of interconnecting triangles.

A strong marriage reflects a triangular shape, composed of each spouse, with God at the apex of the triangle. This configuration is strong, balanced, and capable of maintaining its integrity even if one of you is experiencing a period of weakness or disillusionment.

"A cord of three strands is not easily broken."
Ecclesiastes 4:12 (HCSB)

Not only is this shape strong, but it also establishes a clear path to intimacy. Want to know the secret of getting closer to your mate? **Get closer to God**.

Math Can Save Your Marriage

Remember that morning in Ms McGillicuddy's class when you were day dreaming because math is *super boring*? Remember how frustrated she got and how insistent you were that math is a "waste of time" and you would never actually use it in the "real world"? Well pull up a chair and prepare to eat some crow, because Ms McGillicuddy was right! Math is *extremely important*. In fact...it just might save your marriage.

Many of the problems you are experiencing in your relationship can be solved by implementing proper geometry. To put it simply, your marriage is currently out of shape (see what I did there?).

Irregular Polygon - *The shape of a typical marriage*
When a marriage is shaped as an irregular polygon, it represents an awkward structure with little balance or internal support. In such a marriage, a wide array of issues constantly compete for priority and attention (kids, finances, work, hobbies, etc.), consuming your available

energy in the process. Such a shape is fragile, with some pieces prone to fragmenting and breaking under stress, while other pieces are bloated and unnecessarily enlarged. Tragically, this collection of issues creates a gulf between you and your spouse, introducing barriers to connecting with another and building intimacy.

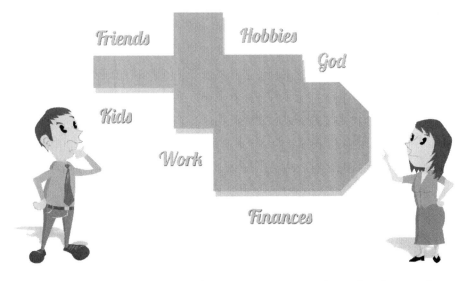

The Irregular Polygon demonstrates a marriage that is out of balance.

Triangle – *The shape of a healthy marriage*
The "Marriage Triangle" offers us a simple illustration of what it means to put your marriage on a firm footing. Notice how the closer you get to the top of the triangle, the shorter the distance is between the two sides? It works the same in your marriage. As each of you draws nearer to God – the source of love and peace, your relationship is brought into balance and the two of you draw closer to each other.

72

Likewise, as you move further away from a daily, intimate relationship with God, the distance from your mate increases as well.

The Marriage Triangle demonstrates a healthy, balanced marriage.

So the question, of course, is which shape best represents <u>your</u> marriage? Do you relate to the changing focus and competing priorities of the irregular polygon, or does your marriage resemble a simple and strong triangle?

More Marriage Math

Geometry is not the only math that is important for your marriage. Ready for some amorous arithmetic? Check out the following:

$$1 + 1 = 1$$

Confused?

$$1 \text{ (Husband)} + 1 \text{ (Wife)} = 1 \text{ (Flesh)}$$

*"For this reason, a man shall leave his father and mother, and the two shall become one flesh; so <u>they are no longer two, but **one flesh**</u>." - Mark 10:7-8*

Ready for another one? Here you go:

$$3 - 1 = 0$$

Just like Ms McGillicuddy taught you, it's important to show your work:

$$3 \text{ (God, You, Your Spouse)} - 1 \text{ (God)} = 0 \text{ (Zip)}$$

*"I am the vine; you are the branches. If you remain in me and I in you, you will bear much fruit; <u>apart from me you can do **nothing**</u>." - John 15:5*

Immense power rests in the combination of these three elements: you, your spouse, and God. Place God as the focus of your relationship and you will experience strength within your marriage and throughout your family you never thought possible. If you take away that source, the critical apex of the triangle, then your marriage will disintegrate. Your marriage can be a success, but you've got to work the numbers a little differently than you might expect.

So as it turns out, Ms McGillicuddy was right; math is super important! It just might save your marriage. And you thought you'd never need geometry after high school.

The Importance of Prayer

One of the primary ways you and your spouse can draw closer to God (and in turn draw closer to each other) is through prayer.

The Skeptical Captain

I heard a story of a ship that was sinking in the middle of a storm, and the captain called out to the crew and said, "Does anyone here know how to pray?"

One man stepped forward and said, "Yes sir, I know how to pray."

The captain said, "Wonderful, you pray while the rest of us put on life jackets – we're one short."

The sad truth is that many people have come to adopt a similar attitude of futility toward prayer. For others, prayer seems foreign, distant, and awkward. But nothing is more important in repairing and rejuvenating your marriage than an active and consistent prayer life.

> **Our marriage** – If we had to point to one factor that played the biggest role in the success of our marriage renewal, it would be prayer. When Tammy and I were re-building our marriage, prayer took center stage. We prayed constantly. For the first 2-3 months we prayed together every night and multiple times throughout the day. Since that time, we have continued a discipline of prayer, praying together 6-7 times a week.

Scripture resonates the theme of communication with the Almighty.

Ask and it will be given to you; seek and you will find; knock and the door will be opened to you. For everyone who asks receives; the one who seeks finds; and to the one who knocks, the door will be opened. – Matt 7:7-8

Submit yourselves, then, to God. Resist the devil, and he will flee from you. Come near to God and He will come near to you. – James 4:7-8

If any of you lacks wisdom, you should ask God, who gives generously to all without finding fault, and it will be given to you. – James 1:5

Jesus is repeatedly seen retreating to a secluded place to seek counsel from his Father. Praying as a couple refreshes your relationship. It preserves your focus on Father God. It soothes fears and hurts. And it unites the two of you in repairing and renewing your marriage.

The Process of Prayer

As children, many of us learned prayer as a formal activity. At pre-determined times (church, meals, and bedtime) you recite a formulaic script you have memorized. But God desires a conversational relationship with his children.

- Prayer doesn't have to be formal – *there's no need for "thee's" and "thou's", we aren't in Medieval times.*

- Prayer doesn't have to be perfect – *don't worry about saying the "right" things or praying the "right way", just talk.*

- Prayer can happen any time for any reason – *you can talk with your Heavenly Father any time for any reason.*

But aren't all the prayers in the Bible formal and elaborate? Aren't there special words you need to say so you can do it "right"?

Nope.

In the Book of Jonah Chapter Two, Jonah is praying to God while inside the belly of the fish. As a part of that prayer, he describes being tossed overboard by the sailors in the previous chapter. Jonah sinks down to the bottom of the sea (v6), he has seaweed wrapped around his head (v5), and his life is fading away as he drowns (v7). In this moment he remembers God and utters a prayer. He doesn't have time for anything formal. He is in no position to think clearly and eloquently. He is desperate and calls out to the Lord in a moment of despair. In spite of this crude, hurried prayer, Jonah was delivered from the giant fish.

Prayer doesn't have to be fancy. In fact, the more raw and authentic, the better. Throughout the Psalms, David pours his heart out expressing his spiritual doubts, his fears, and even his frustrations with the Lord. The more your prayers resemble a conversation with a dear friend, the closer you are getting to the heart of God.

The Content of Prayer

Praying together provides a common point of reference and a shared reminder of your marriage's purpose and identity. Your marriage matters because it is one vital piece of God's overall plan for your family, your community, and your little chunk of the world. But what if you don't know what to say when you pray?

The simple answer is to pray for whatever is on your mind. In the context of your marriage, that means praying together about:

- What worries you

- Things that make you sad

- What you are excited about

- Conflicts you are working through

- Situations where the two of you need wisdom

- Anything for which you are thankful

For a more concrete list, consider the following prayer suggestions for couples.

Twenty-one topics to pray for as a couple

1. A clear vision of your family's future
2. Healing of past hurts
3. Wisdom in building a strong relationship
4. Strength to resist the devil's attempts to attack the relationship
5. Commitment to prioritize the marriage
6. Unity on goals as a couple
7. Peace
8. Quick to hear and slow to anger
9. Hope in a bright future for your union

[continued...]

10. Diligence to continue investing time and energy in building the relationship

11. Faith to not become discouraged during difficult seasons

12. Thankfulness for health

13. Awareness of what God loves about your mate

14. Purpose for your marriage

15. Freedom from bitterness

16. Deeper sexual intimacy

17. Courage to be brutally honest with each other

18. Grace to receive your spouse's honesty

19. Passion to serve in ministry together

20. Gracious eyes to accept each other's faults and short comings

21. Grateful hearts for blessing your marriage with light and love

Your husband/wife is a child of God

Number thirteen from the list ("awareness of what God loves about your mate") holds a special place in my heart and my wife's heart, because it revolutionized our perspective on marriage.

Our marriage – One weekend in February of 2013, Tammy and I attended a marriage conference presented by Dr. David and Teresa Ferguson. We had so many amazing realizations during that conference. The most impactful was this visualization:

"Imagine you are sitting on a rock, next to God, and both of you are gazing a short distance away at your mate. Rather than seeing him or her as your spouse, try to imagine what God sees – His child. Now ask Father God what He loves about His child. What is it about him or her that delights the Father? What special qualities has He uniquely placed within him or her and why did He choose this person to be your soul's mate?"

This exercise transformed our marriage by giving us spiritual eyes to see one another with grace, compassion, and love.

Have you ever thought about that concept? Your spouse is not common, or ordinary, or random. Your mate is a special gift from God. A gift He created and carefully guided through life to grow into the person you needed. This is a precious child of the King of Heaven, and you have been entrusted with the tremendous honor and privilege to love him or her with all your heart and soul. God can't take on flesh and hug your spouse – He needs your arms to embrace His child. God can't physically comfort your mate in times of trouble; He has prepared you to serve as His proxy. God has chosen you as the unique vessel through which He can celebrate and praise and console and encourage and love His son or daughter on this earth. So see your spouse like Jesus does. Ask God to reveal his beloved child to you. And love your husband or wife like crazy, because God is love (I John 4:8) and that's the way He loves you.

The more mature one acts first

Whether you have been married for months, years, or decades, one stalemate plagues nearly every marriage:

- *I'll gladly apologize for calling her "overbearing" as soon as she apologizes for calling me "lazy".*

- *He can give me the silent treatment until the cows come home! I'm not about to apologize for my outburst earlier until he forgives me for being insensitive yesterday.*

- *If she would admit she was wrong, then we could put all of this behind us and move on.*

When relationships reach an impasse like this, moving forward can be very difficult. Both parties are likely to blame, but neither is willing to be the first to extend an olive branch. Each person is so busy being indignantly right, precious time and potential joy is slipping right through their fingers. Worse yet, if the stalemate is never broken, then one or both spouses will translate the undelivered apology into more bitterness and resentment.

So if each shares part of the blame, then how do you possibly break the stalemate? The secret is clarity and maturity. Tammy is fond of saying, "there are three sides to every disagreement: your side, my side, and the truth." *Clarity* means recognizing each of you sees the situation from one perspective. There is validity in each perspective, but the truth is actually somewhere in between. Armed with this knowledge, we consider the second component of breaking a stalemate – *maturity*.

Dr. Emerson Eggerichs, author of *Love and Respect*, has a particularly clever and effective strategy for breaking these sorts of intractable stalemates.

"The more mature one makes the first move."[2]

Wait a second, that's not fair! That means that in order to stay up on my high horse of superiority, I have to humble myself and be the first one to apologize. If I don't, then my spouse gets to be the bigger, more gracious person. That's sneaky! Best of all....it works.

Surround yourself with support

Your environment influences you for better or worse. What you watch, what you listen to, what you read, and who you associate with have a profound impact on your mind and your attitude. So if you and your mate are determined to renew, rebuild, and refresh your marriage, you need to systematically surround yourselves with a support network and resources to equip your marriage for success (we offer some suggestions in Appendix A).

You need motivating and instructive books. Choose positive music and movies. Surround yourselves with encouraging friends and family. You need counselors or mentors to walk alongside you and help your marriage reach its full potential. This issue of your environment shouldn't be taken lightly or addressed halfheartedly, either. There's no room for half-measures or best efforts. It's either "go big, or go home."

---

[2] *Love and Respect* - Dr. Emerson Eggerichs

> **Our marriage** – Creating a positive environment was crucial during our renewal process. I joined a Saturday morning men's Bible study and Tammy found a mentor through Stephen's Ministry. We surrounded ourselves with supportive friends and family. We immersed ourselves in encouraging and even cathartic books, music, seminars, and every other resource we could find. Negative influences were minimized or completely removed. Our marriage's health and vitality became our mission. We poured ourselves completely into the renewal process, crafting a pro-marriage environment.

Your marriage does not need negativity. As you work to repair, renew, and refresh your relationship, you will encounter bitter people. You will find people in your life who have been hurt, resulting in a negative and pessimistic view of marriage. It's said "misery loves company" leading some of these bitter people to drag others down with them, walling in pessimism. You must be careful not to let these people deter you from revitalizing your marriage and transforming it to become all God intends for it to be.

Love is a choice

Romance is delightful, but it is not the embodiment of love. Sexual intimacy in marriage is a beautiful gift from, but it is not the essence of love. Friendship with your mate is a treasure, but you need more than companionship to make a love story.

Renewing and rebuilding your marriage depends upon learning one simple, yet profound truth:

Love is a choice – not a feeling.

When you chose to marry, you chose to bind your life to another. Your futures are intertwined "for richer, for poorer", and "in sickness and in health." Those sacred vows express the selfless endurance that love must be grounded in. The heat and excitement of new love will only sustain you for so long. Lust is temporary. Infatuation is fleeting. Attraction is transient. Eventually, the butterflies in your stomach flutter away as the pressures of "real life" settle in. **Feelings will ebb and flow, but your decision to act lovingly toward your spouse doesn't have to change.**

The love that led Jesus to the cross was an unconditional love of choice (John 15:13). It's not about emotions or circumstances. It's nothing you earn or achieve. The love God has for you and Christ demonstrated on the cross is an all-consuming, selfless love. This is the same love with which husbands are called to love their wives (Ephesians 5:25).

Does this mean you are doomed to live a hollow, emotionless shell of a relationship? By choosing to act lovingly toward your mate, you virtually guarantee the opposite. Psychology has proven through numerous experiments that our hearts will naturally follow our actions. If you doubt this, try forcing yourself to smile consistently for an entire day. Watch how it lifts your spirits and those you encounter. A surprising amount of chemicals and human nature are the real source for your feelings of "love".

Want to know how to *feel* loving toward your mate? Choose to act lovingly. Consistently invest quality time with your husband or wife, and do it with a cheerful attitude and a smile on your face. Deep affection will pour out of your heart as a result of these acts of love. Choose your mate. Choose love. Your heart and all of those long-gone butterflies are sure to follow.

Marriage 2.0 Needs a Solid Foundation

An old adage states: "The best time to plant a tree is 20 years ago. The second best time is today." So it goes with marriage. The beginning of marriage is the best time to establish a rock solid foundation. If you missed that opportunity or have initially assembled a feeble foundation, fear not. No matter how much time has passed, the best course of action is the same. Begin rebuilding your marriage upon a bedrock of trust in God. Do it unequivocally and do it immediately.

The first version of your marriage was clearly lacking. Each of you likely came into the union with some unrealistic expectations. You may have brought with you some bad habits from previous relationships. Perhaps some relationship myths and spiritual warfare have weighed you down. One or both of you may have had a selfish, skewed notion of love and marriage. Now you know more. You've burned your marriage to the ground, and the two of you are committed to working together to rebuild. As you emerge from the ashes of your original, naive version of marriage (what we call "Marriage 1.0") you are now in a position to build your relationship with strength and integrity (the new and improved, "Marriage 2.0"). So don't consider the early years of your marriage a failure, they were merely a beta release that had a few bugs to work out[3].

In this new and improved marriage, commit to build upon this foundation:

- Marriage math with God as the focus

- Consistent prayer together

---

[3]Sorry for all the software references. Sometimes I have to let my nerd flag fly high and proud.

- Gracious hearts eager to apologize and quickly forgive

- A healthy and positive support network and collection of pro-marriage resources

- A firm commitment to love each other with an unconditional, Christ-like love

With a mathematically sound foundation of faith and love, you are ready to begin your journey of renewal.

Chapter Six Reflections

1. Which shape more closely resembles your marriage and its priorities? A triangle or an irregular polygon?

2. Prayer is an important part of marriage renewal. What are practical steps you and your spouse can take to improve your prayer life individually and together?

3. Look back at the "Content of Prayer" section and the list of "Twenty-one topics to pray for as a couple." Write down additional items you would like to pray over.

4. If you had to identify one prayer topic which you consider particularly important for your marriage, what would it be and why?

5. If you went through each day viewing and treating your mate as God's son or daughter, how would it change your thoughts, words, or actions?

6. In "The more mature one acts first" section, two important concepts are introduced: clarity and maturity. How do these help with handling marital conflict?

7. Consider your environment and its impact on your mindset and attitude. Rate the following elements in terms of their influence upon your marriage.

	Very Negative	Somewhat Negative	Somewhat Positive	Very Positive	N/A
Books					
Friends					
Hobbies					
Movies					
Music					
Work					

8. "Feelings will ebb and flow, but your decision to act lovingly toward your spouse doesn't have to change." How would your relationship look different if you fully embraced this truth on a daily basis?

7

Invest in the Relationship

A successful marriage is an edifice that must be
rebuilt every day.

Andre Maurois

Our greatest weakness lies in giving up. The most
certain way to succeed is always to try just one
more time.

Thomas Edison

T HOMAS EDISON CONDUCTED 10,000 experiments in his
effort to perfect the incandescent light. He failed
9,999 times, but his faith and persistence eventually paid
off. I'm not suggesting that your marriage is going to need
10,000 cycles to iron things out, but I am suggesting that
your marriage deserves another chance.

The Renewal Roadmap

Your marriage can be made new again. It can be built
stronger and healthier than ever. Each of you has been hurt
– perhaps very deeply. One or both of you may have

violated the trust in the relationship. This darkness and pain may have lasted a very long time, but there is still hope.

Regardless of your past, your pain, and your problems, God will redeem your marriage and make all things new. He specializes in heart transplants and miraculous renewal (Ezekiel 36:26). With two willing partners and a commitment to dedicate significant time and energy, your marriage can do more than just survive – it can **thrive**.

While the exact course of your renewal will be unique, we have seen patterns emerge in our own journey and the journeys of others we have mentored.

Initially, you need a "no-holds-barred," "go-big-or-go-home" approach to investing in your marriage. You need to break some bad habits and build healthy routines to renew and nurture your relationship. Establish some new patterns, create some new memories, and prioritize your relationship with God and with each other. Over time, the level of engagement can taper down to a more sustainable amount of energy. Renewal will require weeks of intense dedication (Phase One), followed by months of intentional focus (Phase Two), sustained by years of consistent love and attention.

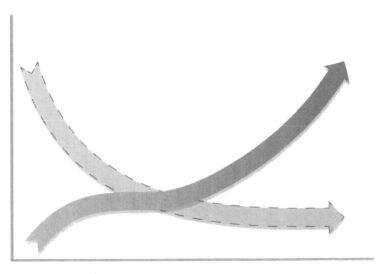

Weeks | Months | Years

Time & Energy Investment
Intimacy and Trust Built

Phase One – The First Forty Days

The first forty days of your marriage renewal are crucial in changing the atmosphere of your relationship and generating the momentum you need to carry you forward. It won't be easy. Breaking patterns and habitual ways of thinking and interacting will prove an enormous challenge. We've chosen forty days, in part, to help you establish new patterns of behavior. Throughout the Bible, forty days has been shown to be a significant time period. Rick Warren's ground-breaking book, *The Purpose-driven Life*, also highlights the efficacy of this length of time. Simply put, a forty day time period allows you to experience an entire month of activity and continue into the next month to maintain the momentum.

Be prepared for significant testing and strain during these first forty days. You may experience raw and unfiltered communication for the first time. You may share hurts and hopes and hang-ups you have kept buried for months or years. You'll almost certainly pour more time and emotional energy into your relationship, and that means other things will have to go on the back-burner for a while. One thing is certain: What you've been doing hasn't been working. It's time to try something new.

Goals for the first forty days

Your aim is to change the atmosphere in your relationship. Re-create the fondness, re-build the friendship, and develop a sense of shared purpose and vision.

During the first forty days, strive to:

- Break old habits (negativity, being critical, isolating yourself, not communicating)

- Establish new patterns and practices (positivity, kindness, openness, thoughtfulness)

- Learn to communicate again (this involves a little bit of talking and a LOT of listening)

- Touch often and find creative ways to connect physically (holding hands, cuddling, light caresses, "bear hugs," light kisses, foot massages, back scratches, passionate kisses, long embraces)

- Be vulnerable (freely share past hurts, current challenges, anything that needs to be worked out)

- Spend purposeful, enjoyable time together (quality time, regular dates, frequent and varied communication)

- Discover your mate's needs (emotional, physical, and spiritual) and discuss how to best meet them

- Learn how to be selfless and truly put your mate's needs before your own

- Temporarily reduce or eliminate non-essential activities (time with friends, hobbies, side projects, optional extra-curricular kid's activities) so you can devote sufficient time toward re-building your relationship

Because your marriage is unique, you and your mate will need to determine your specific goals for the first forty days. As long as you are both in agreement and committed to improving your dynamic, your goals can be as ambitious or conservative as you would like.

Actions for the first forty days

Actions speak louder than words. In fact, when I was re-building trust with Tammy, I told her <u>not</u> to trust my words because they can be misleading. I told her to watch my actions.

Actions flow from the heart and they* never *lie. The actions in which you and your spouse engage are an essential part of re-building your marriage. Create frequent opportunities to spend time together. Talk more, share more, pray more, and experience life together.

Here are some suggestions:

- Daily devotional as a couple (see Appendix A for suggestions) – *provides a natural opportunity to connect, share, and pray*

- Counseling (formal) / mentoring (informal) – *offers insight from a neutral 3rd party and serves as a sounding board*

- Bible study group – *delivers accountability and keeps you focused on your spiritual walk, also can serve as a source of emotional and spiritual support*

- Regular dates – *weekly date nights coupled with mini-dates (lunch, coffee, playing a game together, Slurpees and a walk in the park, etc.)*

- Marriage conference – *serves the dual purpose of time away together while equipping your relationship with valuable tools, techniques, and much-needed insight*

- Do something physically active together – *shared activities promote companionship and boosts your energy and confidence. Examples include exercising together, roller-skating, rock climbing, swimming, and yoga*

- Weekend get-away – *there is no substitute for the refreshing and recharging experience of a weekend away with just the two of you*

- Start a bucket list / "dream book" – *establishes a shared set of goals (places you want to visit, projects you want to start, things you want to learn, experiences you want to have) to help the two of you unite behind a common vision of life*

While we recommend doing as much together as you can during the first forty days, some of your work should also be independent. The wife might meet have coffee with a mentor while the husband attends a weekly men's small group through church. One of you might be in a support group while the other attends a weekly Bible study. A blend of shared activities and solo support activities provides valuable insight from external parties.

Additionally, you'll want to take the advice given in the previous chapter, placing prayer at the center of your relationship and surrounding yourself with a supportive environment. Immerse your relationship in a flood of love and attention and begin to grow stronger roots to withstand the inevitable dry seasons.

Phase Two – Healing and Rebuilding

Your first forty days were likely a roller-coaster of emotion, intimacy, and vulnerability. Many couples get caught up in the energy and the excitement of breathing new life into their marriage. However, the critical season following those first forty days will determine whether these changes will last or if the couple will slip back into old patterns and behaviors.

This challenging second phase of renewal will force you to more deeply process past hurts and problems. The initial excitement and enthusiasm of renewal has subsided, but you still have a lot of emotions to process. You may be working through the same issues, but at another level of depth. Or you may be working through issues that you have been ignoring up until now. In any case, you will need to continue to prioritize the time and energy necessary to resolve any conflict or complication that arises. Digging up all of these hurts and hang-ups will not be easy. By ignoring them and burying them, you were able to quickly cope. This alleviated stress initially, but leaving issues unresolved sets up your marriage for heartbreak in the long term. By unpacking all of this baggage, you will force yourselves to re-visit some painful places in your past. You have to completely work through this pain in order to move your relationship forward. Renewal is challenging, exhausting, and even frightening, but well worth the effort.

In uncovering these wounds, expect to experience a cycle of emotions fairly rapidly (hope, frustration, joy, anger, etc.). This is normal. Best of all, as you work together to heal the broken places in each other's hearts, you'll plant the seeds for a deep and lasting bond.

Goals for the second phase

With your initial forty-day investment behind you, you are ready for the next phase of renewal. Begin to fold more of your regular activities back into your routine while still maintaining your top two priorities: closeness with your Heavenly Father and closeness with His beloved child, your spouse.

Together, consider the following goals for this stage:

- Keep God at the center of your relationship (pray daily as a couple, serve in a ministry together, seek relationship wisdom in scripture)

- Maintain a commitment to prioritizing your relationship (regular date nights, daily time spent talking and connecting authentically, meals together, tokens of love)

- Continue to talk through challenges and obstacles as a team (open and honest communication, patience, and understanding)

- Avoid falling back into old patterns (taking the relationship for granted, retreating to isolation, avoiding conflict)

- Find a sustainable balance between your newly prioritized relationship and previously tabled activities (hobbies, side projects, extra time with friends, optional kid's activities, etc.)

- Elevate each other's needs above your own (sacrifice time / money / convenience)

As before, the goals you select should be collaboratively chosen by you and your spouse. Even if you choose to use some or all of the goals identified here, the two of you may decide what elements of each goal to pursue.

Actions for the second phase

Your actions during the second phase of renewal should mirror the activities from the first forty days, but also reflect a deepening of your relationship and your intimacy.

The list of actions you could incorporate is extensive, but the following should serve as useful examples:

- Read a book together (see Appendix A for suggestions) – *creates an opportunity to discuss and share ideas (couple's devotional, relationship book, or something else you are both interested in reading)*

- Counseling / mentoring – *an invaluable resource to help in healing the past hurts and hang-ups that so often surface during this stage of renewal*

- Ministry project – *volunteer together in your local community or through a global ministry*

- Regular dates – *this will continue to be a critical activity, but you'll likely find a need to adjust the frequency in order to accommodate realistic time constraints*

- Relationship-building events – *helps to build communication and relationship skills (marriage conferences, Bible studies at church, small group studies, weekend retreats)*

- Joint project – *plan an activity that requires joint preparation and shared work (start a garden, train for a run or bike ride, raise money for a cause you both believe in, renovate a room of your house)*

- Frequent check-ins (see Appendix A for suggestions) – *establish a pattern for consistent communication to identify issues requiring resolution before they become a problem*

In this second phase, vigilantly protect and maintain your progress and leverage it to grow closer to God and closer to one another. One important theme for this phase is to identify one or more projects that the two of you can work on as a team. In particular, look for opportunities to serve in your community or church together. Renowned author and blogger, Jen Hatmaker, remarks: "Generosity has the power to heal." This sentiment is echoed in Isaiah 58:6-8 (NLT).

This is the kind of fasting I want:

Free those who are wrongly imprisoned;

lighten the burden of those who work for you.

Let the oppressed go free,

and remove the chains that bind people.

Share your food with the hungry,

and give shelter to the homeless.

Give clothes to those who need them,

and do not hide from relatives who need your help.

Then your salvation will come like the dawn,

and your wounds will quickly heal.

Let this prayer serve as a blessing over your renewal process – *"your salvation will come like the dawn, and your wounds will quickly heal."*

Rebuilding Trust

Prior to beginning this renewal process, your spiritual and emotional connection had faded and your bond had weakened. While this will look different for each couple, the simple fact is this: *trust has been broken at some level.* In most cases, the trust has been broken by both the husband and wife. You trusted your mate to love you fully and selflessly, and he or she fell short of that mark. In more extreme situations, you find yourself coping with betrayal of trust from addiction, abuse, or infidelity. Wherever you are on the spectrum, trust has been violated, and rebuilding it will require time and patience. It won't be easy, but take heart, *trust can be restored.*

Listed below are guidelines for restoring trust. Many of these apply equally to both parties, while others are specific to the spouse that is working to rebuild the trust (the *trust healer*) or the spouse that is learning to trust again (the *hurting spouse*).

Guidelines for rebuilding trust in your relationship

- **Be patient** *(both of you)* – There is no timetable for rebuilding trust. Intimate business of forgiveness and trust require an unknown amount of time to accomplish. Don't rush this process.

- **Be open** *(both of you)* – Communicate early (before a problem can escalate) and often (as frequently as an issue occurs). Share your hearts with one another and be vulnerable in expressing your doubts and fears.

- **Be reliable** *(trust healer)* – Under-promise and over-deliver. Don't make hasty, unrealistic commitments. Instead, let your word be your bond and overwhelm your spouse with your consistency and predictability.

- **Be humble** *(trust healer)* – Pride is the enemy of trust. You must empty yourself of ego and be willing to take any measures necessary to heal the brokenness (formal apologies, schedule changes, job changes, routine changes, etc.).

- **Be receptive** *(hurting spouse)* – You must be receptive to the work that God wants to do in your heart. You also need to be open to receiving love from your spouse and accept his or her efforts to demonstrate trustworthiness.

- **Be understanding** *(trust healer)* – Recognize that your spouse is hurt and those wounds will take time and constant reassurance to heal. Furthermore, the healing process may go in cycles. There will be good days and bad days, but be compassionate and understanding throughout.

- **Be courageous** *(both of you)* – It is tempting to give into fear and doubt, to assume that one or both of your will break the trust again. It is tempting to believe that the outlook is hopeless. Resist all of this negativity. Be optimistic and courageous.

- **Be expectant** *(both of you)* – Expect God to reveal Himself powerfully. Put your faith in Him and expect that He will meet both of you more than half-way. You aren't in this alone. The God of Heaven is in your corner and will bless your marriage with the peace and understanding you need to re-establish confidence.

Once trust has been broken, it is difficult – but not impossible – to restore. As Jesus said, "With God all things are possible" (Matthew 19:26).

Wounds Heal Crooked

The process of healing deep wounds of the heart is messy. There is no script and no timeline. As the wounds heal, you pass through cycles of hope and doubt, cycles of peace and conflict. There are cycles of anger, cycles of joy, and cycles of heartache. As one or both of you experience the painful side of these emotional swells, it may feel as though you have lost ground. Your intimacy may suffer. Your connection may temporarily weaken. **This is normal**. The healing process isn't neat or tidy. Renewal is a broken, jagged path.

Sometimes it isn't the natural cycle of emotions that you combat, but the looming reminders. A song, a smell, or a statement may launch you back to a time in your relationship's past when you were hurt. Memories of past statements or events may haunt you. Your marriage is especially vulnerable to this when you are in the process of rebuilding trust. Selfish actions or inconsiderate statements by the *trust breaker* may cause past hurts to flood back into your mind. It may feel as if you are experiencing the pain all over again. The key to overcoming this uninvited ghost from your past, is for the trust breaker to transition into the role of trust healer (described earlier). This is a shift in mindset, attitude, and actions. Both of you must briefly visit the past to heal wounds that arise. You can't live there however. Heal the wound, give it God, and then turn your attention to the present. Dwell in your renewed relationship, not the remnants of your old one.

As the two of you weather these emotional storms, it is important to maintain your perspective in a few key areas:

- Experiencing pain and anger from the past at multiple (and even random) times throughout the renewal process is normal.

- Neither of you is perfect. Expect some inconsiderate statements, moments of selfishness, and other demonstrations of human frailty during the renewal process.

- Two steps forward and one step back is still progress.

- It is natural for emotional pain to be processed and resolved multiple times before it is fully healed.

- Anytime there is a momentary setback in your renewal, the correct response is always *grace*.

While grace and love must flow freely in your marriage, this should never be used as an excuse for poor choices. Each of you must still accept responsibility for your own actions. When your renewal process has setbacks, it is important to quickly and genuinely apologize to one another.

Our marriage – Throughout our renewal, we have had our share of setbacks.

- Periodically, I have made inconsiderate statements or attempted to break the tension with inappropriate jokes about our past.

- Month 2, 6, 17 and 18: Tammy felt exhausted from the constant mental warfare as the enemy continued to remind her of the past.

- Month 3, 5, 9, and 12: I felt held down by the weight of my guilt and shame.

- Month 4 and 10: I wrestled with doubts as to whether or not we could really overcome our past.

- Month 5 and 14: Tammy lit into me in a fit of anger and ripped me up one side and down the other.

Whatever pain may exist in your marriage, take courage. While nothing has been done can ever be undone, broken hearts and broken lives can be mended. The process isn't clean, it isn't easy, and it isn't quick. Healing is messy and crooked. It takes time, energy, and mountains of patience. But keep pressing on because your marriage can overcome heartache. Your heart can heal. Your soulmate's heart can heal. Your marriage can heal. Best of all, when you go on that journey of healing together, your bond grows stronger than it ever was before. Scar tissue isn't pretty, but it is resilient. Embrace the crooked journey and love each other like crazy.

Making the Renewal Last

A third phase of renewal occurs after you rekindle your bond. We like to call this phase "daily renewal." It's equal parts relationship maintenance, healing of hurts, and marital bliss. You aren't plagued with doubts, hurts, and fears as often; yet, it would be foolish to expect that you'll never have to face those ghosts from the past at some point. Likewise, new pains will surface and these must also be addressed with care. We call this *daily renewal* because each day, you must make up your mind to renew your love, renew your passion, and renew your commitment to honor each other with your thoughts, words, and actions.

There's no predicting when your relationship will enter this final, on-going phase of renewal. Its timing depends upon your collective history and how much pain there is to heal. Couples with relatively little to repair may reach this phase within six months. We've seen some couples with significant pain (infidelity, addictions, etc.) requiring a year or more before this stage. Regardless of when you reach it, this third phase reflects a certain rhythm. There may still be cyclical emotions to process, and you will inevitably experience "seasons" of death and renewal within your relationship. Physical pain can heal relatively easily, but emotional wounds often must heal in layers. Sometimes those layers of healing and pain processing occur over weeks or months while others can take years. The frequency and intensity of anger and pain should have diminished considerably during this third phase.

Your marriage is a marathon, not a sprint. While we recommend an initial concentrated burst of activity during the first forty days, that intensity tapers during the second phase. Eventually, during the third phase, you aim for a more sustainable level of engagement so you can continue to invest in your marriage over the long haul. The key to success is building healthy patterns of communication and shared experiences to further strengthen your bond. We will explore strategies for successfully maintaining these new patterns and behaviors in Section III, "Beauty Out of Ashes."

Thomas Edison was a relentless optimist. He constantly wondered what he could accomplish with one more try, one more experiment. You might not be perfecting the light bulb or automating the telegraph, but restoring your marriage is no less important. God has a unique and beautiful vision for your marriage and how it fits into the Kingdom. Don't you think that deserves one more shot?

Chapter Seven Reflections

1. Phase One – The First Forty Days

    a. Identify <u>goals</u> for your initial phase of renewal

    b. Identify <u>actions</u> you can take to renew your marriage

2. Phase Two – Healing and Rebuilding

    a. Identify <u>goals</u> for your second phase of renewal

    b. Identify <u>actions</u> you can sustain during this phase

3. Rebuilding trust is challenging. For most couples there are at least a few minor areas which require trust to be rebuilt (hurt feelings or unmet needs). For others, there may be substantial damage (abuse, neglect, or an affair) necessitating a trust to be rebuilt from scratch.

In what ways does trust need to be rebuilt in your relationship?

4. Wounds don't heal in nice, clean lines. Wounds heal crooked. They require love and patience. It may take multiple healing sessions over months or years.

What can you do to be sensitive to the healing process within your mate?

Remember: God has a unique and beautiful vision for your marriage and how it fits into the Kingdom. Pray over your relationship and ask for clarity regarding the mission for your marriage.

8

Combating the Enemy

If you know the enemy and know yourself, you need not fear the result of a hundred battles.

Sun Tzu
The Art of War

S PORTS TEAMS WATCH HOURS OF FOOTAGE to better understand their opponents. Boxers and martial artists study the fighting style and techniques employed by their competitors. Military commanders carefully analyze their enemy's tactics, patterns, and strategies in order to prepare for battle. Likewise, knowledge of your opposition and preparation based upon that knowledge is a crucial success factor in your marriage. So it is important that you **know** your enemy, **prepare** yourself for battle, and **establish cues** to remind you of the warfare all around you and keep you grounded in truth.

Know your Enemy

Realize who is at war against your marriage – and no, it is not your spouse. Scripture is quite clear that your Enemy is the devil and his minions (I Peter 5:8 and Ephesians 6:12). As we explored in Chapter 4, attacking marriages is an extremely efficient way to destroy families and ultimately to nullify the overall impact of the church and the kingdom.

Paul reminds us in Ephesians that we are at war against those forces that are unseen:

For our battle is not against flesh and blood, but against the rulers, against the authorities, against the world powers of this darkness, against the spiritual forces of evil in the heavens. – Ephesians 6:12 (HCSB)

Armed with this knowledge, it is important to evaluate disagreements, frustrations, arguments, and obstacles in your relationship through a spiritual filter. The enemy would love nothing more than to capitalize on these conflicts and use them as a way to drive a wedge between the two of you. He plants a seed of doubt or frustration and nurtures it over time. That aggravation grows in your mind, like a tree root digging deep, sprawling and twisting toward a house. Left untended, it will break apart the foundation of that house. Likewise, if you and your spouse are not vigilant, the seeds of doubt and frustration in your marriage will grow until they create a rift in your relationship. This danger is never more real than once you commit to rebuilding your marriage. Be on the alert.

Navigating the mental battlefield

Recognizing that the enemy works to prevent your marriage from succeeding is just the beginning. Being aware of the tools that the enemy will use against you and your spouse is the first step in your battle plan.

The enemy preys upon base and negative human emotions like fear, pride, selfishness, and greed (I John 2:16). By contrast, your Heavenly Father employs faith, hope, and love (I Corinthians 13:13). The trouble is that all of this is taking place between your ears. It is a battlefield of the mind!

Our thoughts and feelings consume us all day long. This is particularly true if you and your spouse are currently working to resolve a dispute. How can you possibly know if your thoughts originate from the proverbial angel or devil on your shoulder? Jesus said: "By their fruit you will recognize them." (Matthew 7:16). While he was talking about how to recognize faithful people, the principle is applicable in this context as well. Look for the *fruit* or outcome of your thought process.

When working through an issue with your spouse, reflect on the core emotion driving your thoughts. Dig deep. Reflect. Pray. If you find that your thoughts are dominated by fear and doubt, it is reasonable to attribute that preoccupation to the enemy. First John 4:18 promises "perfect love drives out fear" – the fear consuming you is not a heaven-sent tool. Your gracious and loving Dad in heaven won't give you a steady diet of fear or lead you to dwell on bitterness and resentment. Instead, his tools are love and grace.

Consider the following table:

Satan's Tools (various verses)	God's Tools (Galatians 5:22)
• Fear • Doubt • Bitterness • Resentment • Anger • Pride • Manipulation • Selfishness	• Love • Joy • Peace • Patience • Kindness • Goodness • Faithfulness • Gentleness • Self-control

This doesn't mean every time you experience fear or doubt in your relationship that the devil is attacking you. Many of these negative words are normal and valid human emotions. Simply be cautious of the tendency to dwell on such emotions. If you find yourself consumed by the emotions on the left, you have fallen into the clever and patient hands of the enemy.

Knowing the enemy and how he operates is only *half* the battle. Marriage is not a spectator's sport. You must **train your mind and prepare your heart** for battle. You'll be fighting for your spouse, your marriage, and your family.

> **Our marriage** – One night, early in our renewal process, Tammy and I were having a raw heart-to-heart conversation. She was consumed with fear that our relationship would not be able to heal. It was plaguing her with doubt and robbing her of joy. In a moment of clarity, scripture came to my mind – "Perfect love casts out fear" (I John 4:18), and I realized Tammy was under attack! We talked through it, drew near to Dad in prayer and started a new chapter in our walk. From that night forward, we both began to see more clearly the threat and reality of spiritual warfare and its impact on our marriage.

Prepare Yourself for Battle

Victory goes to the prepared. Abraham Lincoln was known to put a premium on preparation: "If I had eight hours to chop down a tree, I'd spend six sharpening my axe."

Preparation for spiritual warfare is crucial:

- In the Old Testament, the children of Israel prepared for battle with a blessing and encouragement from a priest (Deuteronomy 20:1-4).

- Jesus didn't begin his ministry until he was thirty. He spent three decades preparing for a three-year-long ministry.

- Jesus fasted forty days before he was led into the wilderness to be tempted by Satan (Matthew 4:1-11).

- Early church elders fasted before sending missionaries out to preach (Acts 13:1-3).

Preparation for battle requires time, as well as mentor and physical conditioning (Luke 3:23).

The Armor of God

"Finally, be strong in the Lord and in his mighty power. Put on the full armor of God, so that you can take your stand against the devil's schemes." – Ephesians 6:10-11

As a child, I recall learning about "the armor of God" (Ephesians 6) in Sunday school. We would color pictures of soldiers, sing songs, and memorize the different pieces of armor and what they represent. It always made for fun visuals. Years later, I truly appreciated the metaphor expressed in Ephesians 6:10-18 and what preparation for spiritual battle is really about.

- *"Belt of truth" (v.14)* – truth is a powerful defense against the lies the Enemy will use in an effort to drive a wedge between you and your mate.

- *"Breastplate of righteousness" (v.14)* – your identity in Jesus Christ enables you to overcome your faults and failures and live a new life of purpose.

- *"Shield of faith" (v.16)* – the process of repairing and renewing your marriage won't be an easy one; you're going to need your faith to protect you during spiritual attacks on your marriage.

- *"Helmet of salvation" (v.17)* – the ultimate protection for your mind is your identity as a redeemed and loved child, saved by God's grace.

- *"Sword of the spirit, which is the word of God" (v.17)* – filling your mind with the truth and wisdom of scripture will provide you peace in times of doubt as well as ammunition during direct attacks.

Finally, verse 18 encourages Christian soldiers to "pray in the Spirit on all occasions." Prayer is the bonding agent that forges your spiritual armor together, equipping you for battle.

Establish cues to maintain focus

Fighting a battle or two when you are prepared for it isn't a big deal. But vigilantly managing your thoughts throughout each day will exhaust you. You will need to remain focused on what is true and what is false.

For though we live in the world, we do not wage war as the world does. The weapons we fight with are not the weapons of the world. On the contrary, they have divine power to demolish strongholds. We demolish arguments and every pretension that sets itself up against the knowledge of God, and we take captive every thought to make it obedient to Christ. – II Corinthians 10:3-5

The real battlefield is a battlefield of the mind. You must constantly wage war against the strongholds within your mind and within your spouse's mind. The enemy will attempt to rationalize and justify your anger, your fear, your bitterness, and your resentment. You must respond to such attacks with faith and a renewed commitment to your marriage. Each time the enemy attempts to separate you from your beloved, you must respond by taking that invitation toward negativity and making that thought "obedient toward Christ."

Lies about your marriage

- Your spouse doesn't care about you or your needs.

- Some relationships just aren't meant to work out.

- There is too much pain and bitterness for your renewal to succeed.

- Making a fresh start with someone else would be easier.

- If your spouse would change, then everything would be better.

Truths about your marriage

- You and your spouse are both children of God.

- Your marriage can be renewed and refreshed.

- God chose your mate as a gift for you.

- Your marriage's success has a divine purpose.

- God can save any marriage.

The renewal of your relationship depends upon your ability to reject the lies of the enemy and hold firm to the truths of your marriage. To do that, establish reminders that your mind is engaged in an ongoing spiritual battle.

- Memorize scripture.

- Keep scripture and encouraging quotes on note cards and keep them in places you will see them.

- Christians have used physical reminders for centuries (prayer beads, prayer bracelets, some even feel comfortable getting tattoos).

- Set visual reminders such as pictures of armor or weapons.

- Find encouraging songs and listen to them repeatedly.

- Engage social media for reminders and tips. Join marriage-building Facebook groups and follow pro-marriage feeds on Twitter (see Appendix A for suggested resources).

Remember, while the tangible world preoccupies you, an on-going spiritual war will engulf your marriage if you do not remain vigilant. My favorite passage regarding spiritual warfare comes from II Kings. In chapter two, we are introduced to the prophet Elisha. Elisha's prophecies and support of the Israelite army had landed him as public enemy #1 of the King of Aram. One morning, Elisha and his servant awake to find their city surrounded by an Aramean army. II Kings 6:15-17 (HCSB) paints the picture.

> *When the servant of the man of God got up early and went out, he discovered an army with horses and chariots surrounding the city. So he asked Elisha, "Oh, my master, what are we to do? "*
>
> *Elisha said, "Don't be afraid, for those who are with us outnumber those who are with them."*
>
> *Then Elisha prayed, "LORD, please open his eyes and let him see." So the LORD opened the servant's eyes. He looked and saw that the mountain was covered with horses and chariots of fire all around Elisha.*

No matter what challenges your marriage may face, you have a protector. – *"Don't be afraid, for those who are with us outnumber those who are with them."*

You Can Overcome

Wouldn't it be great if you could learn about your opponent the same way that sports teams do in advance of a game? You can. Scripture is full of examples of how the enemy attacks individuals, families, and nations. Study these stories and learn about your enemy like a military commander preparing for battle. Take courage, because the whole host of heaven is rallied around the two of you to support, encourage, and defend your beautiful bond of matrimony. Through Christ, your marriage can overcome anything this world throws at you. Hang on, pray daily, and never allow the enemy to exchange truth for lies.

Chapter Eight Reflections

1. Which of Satan's tools (fear, doubt, bitterness, resentment, anger, pride, manipulation, selfishness) most often robs your marriage of joy?

2. Which of God's tools (love, joy, peace, patience, kindness, goodness, faithfulness, gentleness, self-control) would make the biggest impact in your marriage and why?

3. "The Armor of God" highlights several key elements to prepare for spiritual warfare.

    a. With which piece of armor are you most comfortable?

    b. With which element of armor are you most vulnerable?

    c. In which element of armor does your mate most need your prayers and support?

4. The real battlefield is in your mind. You must be vigilant and sift through the nonsense to see the truth from lies.

a. What lies do you believe about your marriage?

b. What truths do you need to embrace?

5. Many people find it helpful to establish cues to remind them of the mental battlefield (*memorize scripture, quote cards, tattoos, visual reminders, encouraging songs/playlists, and targeted social media*).

What cues can you establish to prepare and maintain your mindset?

Remember: The renewal of your relationship depends upon your ability to reject the lies of the enemy and hold firm to the truths of your marriage.

Section III

Beauty out of Ashes

*Enjoying and protecting the gift of
your renewed relationship*

9

Fortify Your Marriage

Coming together is a beginning; keeping together is progress; working together is success.

Henry Ford

ONE SUMMER MY PARENTS asked me to convert one of our long-neglected flower beds into a vibrant garden. While it sounds simple enough, this was a very large area that had been ignored for years. It was completely overgrown with vines, a few struggling weeds, and smothered in layers of oak leaves (robbing the soil of water and sun). Clearing the bed of vines and debris took nearly two days, but the real work began once I started to dig. After about half an inch of soil, I hit pure Texas clay. It might as well have been concrete. I used a pick ax for days to break up the clay and burrow the 8+ inches needed to support the root systems of the new leafy green residents. Following that, I spent a couple of weeks mixing in top soil, hoeing, folding in peat moss, watering, and raking the bed of debris. Terraforming clay into viable soil is no small task.

Finally, after nearly six weeks, the bed was suitable for planting begonias, caladiums, hydrangeas, and a smattering of other colorful flora.

The end result of my effort was stunning, but also a bit anti-climactic. When I think about that flower bed, it's easy for me to take pride in the blood and sweat I sacrificed to rescue the bed. Breaking through that clay with a pick axe and painstakingly converting it into healthy soil gave me a clear sense of accomplishment. But that was just the beginning. For years afterwards, I continued the onerous work of maintaining that flower bed. Maintenance isn't particularly gratifying or impressive; it's laborious. Sustaining a garden, day after day and week after week, is mentally taxing. Remaining vigilant is a challenge when heroic effort is no longer required. The initial excitement gives way to tedium.

Your Relationship is like a Garden

Imagine your relationship as a garden. This may terrify you if your thumbs are far from green and you tend to kill anything bearing leaves. But when it comes to relationships, I think we are all a bit clueless as to how to effectively tend our marital gardens. Like anything worthwhile, it doesn't come quickly or easily.

In Chapter 7, we walked through the process of renewing your marriage. The first forty days required intense and focused effort, like breaking through the clay of a flower bed. The second phase of your renewal is an emotionally tender season. You must be diligent to nurture your connection and strengthen your foundation, much like rebuilding the bed with top soil and peat moss. Finally, you plant shrubs and flowers and enjoy all of your effort. But this ushers in a new phase that requires commitment and determination. You and your spouse must maintain what you have built and continually refresh your marital bond.

Feed your Garden

It may not be glamorous, but your marital garden must be fed daily. No fanfare, no impressive overtures – just diligent investments of time and energy to strengthen your relationship's roots and branches.

Sources of nourishment

- **Your environment** – The people you associate with, the pace and temperament of your home, and the overall tone of your environment will either nourish or poison your marriage. Does your work environment create peace or stress? Is your home a sanctuary or a sanitarium? Do you associate with positive, encouraging people, or are you surrounded with drama and negativity? Who in your corner genuinely supports your restored marriage?

Whoever walks with the wise becomes wise, but the companion of fools will suffer harm. – Proverbs 13:20

Do not be deceived: "Bad company corrupts good morals." – 1 Corinthians 15:33

- **Your content** – "Oh be careful little eyes what you see...oh be careful little ears what you hear..." – as children we learned to guard our hearts and minds by guarding our eyes and ears. What you choose to expose yourself to on a regular basis profoundly impacts your thoughts and attitude. You can't spiritually binge at church once a week and then try to live off of that for six days. You need a steady diet of scripture, prayer, and journaling. The music you listen to and the books you read affect your outlook on life, and thus your marriage.

Consider what David writes in Psalm 101:

> *I will sing of faithful love and justice;*
> *I will sing praise to You, Lord.*
> *I will pay attention to the way of integrity.*
> *When will You come to me?*

I will live with a heart of integrity in my house.

I will not set anything worthless before my eyes.

I hate the practice of transgression;

  it will not cling to me.

A devious heart will be far from me.

I will not be involved with evil.[4]

In the New Testament, Paul exhorts the Philippians to focus their minds on things that are honorable and true.

Finally brothers, whatever is true, whatever is honorable, whatever is just, whatever is pure, whatever is lovely, whatever is commendable--if there is any moral excellence and if there is any praise--dwell on these things.-- Philippians 4:8

- **Your accountability** – Establishing sources of counsel and accountability will provide guidance to your renewed relationship. It may be a small group at church, or a mentor with whom you meet over coffee, or an older couple who imparts wisdom and insight. Accountability assures you

---

[4] Psalm 101:1-4

and your spouse are not on your own. You need guidance. You need truth delivered to you in love. You need others holding you and your spouse accountable for investing in your marriage.

Where there is no guidance, a people falls, but in an abundance of counselors there is safety. – *Proverbs 11:14 (ESV)*

Consistently feeding your mind and hearing encouraging messages will boost your resolve to preserving your revitalized marriage. A supportive environment, effective and positive use of your time, and accountability through wise counsel are essential to nourishing your marital garden.

Protect your Garden

Feeding your relationship is important, but none of that matters if you allow insects and vermin to devour the new marriage you have built. As we have already explored, we face a tremendous foe who wages a spiritual battle for our hearts and minds. The enemy will never stop until your marriage has been completely destroyed. Never forget – the enemy is patient and cunning. As you commit to cultivating your refreshed relationship, you must prepare for the inevitable battle that awaits you.

The enemy will attempt to prey upon your spouse's doubts, fears, and insecurities. If he can drive a wedge between the two of you, then he has won. Don't allow an opening that the devil can exploit.

Any division he can create weakens the power of your relationship. Since so much of the battleground is found in your minds, protect your spouse's mind and heart from the lies of the enemy should take top priority.

The enemy will twist and contort any situation, any frustration, and any disagreement in an effort to divide the two of you. Consequently, you must counteract the lies with truth and with love.

> **Our marriage** – Throughout our healing and renewal process, we have battled doubts and fears. Through those experiences, we have learned the importance of being proactive and doing everything in our power to encourage and reassure each other. We plant positive thoughts in one another's heart, speak encouraging words, and pray on one another's behalf. Teamwork is essential.

You must be proactive. Talk frequently. Offer reassurance. Freely and openly speak words of affirmation. Treat one another with respect and shower each other with unconditional love. You can't leave room for doubt in the mind of your spouse. Under-promise, over-deliver, and communicate to a fault. Protect the beautiful friendship and bond of love you have built. This is not the time to get lazy.

Tend your Garden

Strong marriages are not accidental. They require continual investments of time and energy. You must pay attention to emotions (yours and your mates) and create shared experiences. Above all, you must communicate constantly and create a safe, healthy environment for your marriage to thrive. Don't be afraid to set boundaries, limiting interaction with negative people, reducing time spent away from each other, or adjusting your social calendar to prioritize your relationship. The structure of your life will significantly impact the long-term strength and well-being of your marriage.

Gardening requires frequent attention to ensure your plants and flowers have everything they need. Similarly, your marriage needs frequent check-ins to identify unresolved unmet needs.

There are many check-in techniques you can employ:

- **Daily Review** – Praying together each night affords a unique opportunity to examine the day, decompress, and connect spiritually in prayer. To expand the conversation, try sharing the best and worst parts of your day. This simple technique effectively promotes reflection and opens a dialogue.

- **Weekly Status Meetings** – One hour each week, "check in" and see how things are going. Discuss disagreements, miscommunications, things you are thankful for, and how to more effectively meet each other's needs. For more details, check out the "Weekly Staff Meeting" technique (see Appendix A).

- **Tank Check** – Periodically, as needed, you ask each other how your "'love tank" is doing. This technique from *Love and Respect* (see Appendix A) aims to establish a simple means of gauging how "full" your heart feels with loving deposits made by your mate. Identify on a scale of one to ten, how loved you feel. Anything less than a seven warrants a discussion to uncover opportunities for improvement.

These techniques will enable you to develop a predictable means of touching base and uncovering the status of your relationship.

As you tend your marital garden, be mindful of the following:

- **Water your garden** - The grass isn't greener "on the other side," it's greener where you water it. A thriving, fulfilling marriage requires nourishing time and energy. Water your garden with love, water it with respect, water it with quality time, water it with affection, and do all of this watering *together*.

- **Pull out weeds early and often** – Weeds choke your plants and starve your grass of precious nutrients. The weeds in your marital garden are toxic relationships and negative influences. Your single friends who want to hang out at bars and hit on women. Your bitter aunt who assumes the worst in every situation. While you may not be able to eliminate all these people from your lives, you and your spouse should minimize exposure to negative, toxic relationships.

- **Gardens need good, nutrient-rich soil** – No amount of water and weed pulling will get you anywhere if you don't have healthy soil. Feed yourself a healthy diet of positive and encouraging books, music, prayer, and journaling. Likewise, feed your mate a healthy diet of love and respect. Learn your spouse's love language and make consistent deposits in his or her "love bank."

- **The enemy is good at hiding** – Gardens have many hidden foes from burrowing ground hogs to minuscule insects. They are sneaky and treacherous. Likewise, the primary enemy of your marriage is crafty and able to avoid detection, while still chipping away at the bond between you and your mate. Keep your guard up and defend your marriage with vigilance!

You Can't Coast Forever

As I became increasingly busy in the latter years of high school, that flower bed received less and less care. My priorities changed, and eventually I stopped maintaining it altogether. The bed gradually returned to its previous neglected state – but not overnight because the investment I had made afforded some residual benefits.

The same is true with your relationship. You may not notice at first because you can 'coast' on the loving deposits you have already made. But eventually you will have made too many withdrawals and will have neglected your marital garden for too long.

Without vigilant attention, your garden will begin to die. But that doesn't have to be your story. Choose to grow your own happily ever after.

Chapter Nine Reflections

1. Like a garden, your relationship needs nourishment. Your marriage is nourished through your environment, the content you consume, and trusted individuals and couples that can serve as mentors. What changes can you make to nourish your marriage?

2. You must battle for your mate's mind. Renewal is hard. Each day could hold doubts, fears, and pain from the past. Be proactive and bless your spouse with love and attention. Identify ways you can protect your spouse's mind.

3. Tend your Garden. Your relationship requires daily care.

   a. What can you do to "check in" regularly?

   b. What else can you do to care for your marriage?

10

Enjoy Your Time Together

A successful marriage requires falling in love many times, always with the same person.

Mignon McLaughlin

T HE FIRST NIGHT TAMMY AND I MET, we parlayed a quick meeting over coffee into an extended dinner (the waiter kicked us out when the restaurant closed), and eventually we ended up at the observation area of DFW airport, talking for hours as planes flew overhead. Hours felt like minutes, and we couldn't get enough of each other. Since that first night, we have spent many magical days exploring Highway 1 in California, braving sub-arctic temperatures at Winterlude in Ottawa, dining in the dark while being served by blind waiters in Montreal, drinking strawberry mojitos on the beach in Barcelona, and zip-lining in Jamaica. While we can't predict memorable moments, we aim to create a ripe environment by being open-minded, adventurous, and willing to step outside of our respective comfort zones. Most importantly, we have committed to prioritizing time with just the two of us.

Never Stop Courting

In September 2009, I sent Tammy on a scavenger hunt all over the Dallas/Fort Worth metroplex. This hunt included destinations in four cities, incorporating appetizers, coffee, a custom fortune cookie, a walk through the park where we first kissed, multiple handwritten notes with clues, and a singing gondolier who rowed us through the canals in Las Colinas, and a multi-course dinner served to us as we glided through the canals. Finally, at sunset, our gondolier fished a bottle out of the canal and placed it on the table in front of us. Tammy pulled out the note and read aloud a love letter I had written her. When she finished the letter, I asked her to marry me, and we kissed as the sun set over the canal (oh, and one more thing – she totally said "yes").

That date was magical and Hollywood-worthy, the result of days of planning and preparation. Fast forward a couple years to a mountain of bills and schedules, work and school activities, exhaustion and stress. The couple who was so very much in love had embarked upon a passionate adventure, only to become overwhelmed with the pace of life and the responsibilities of managing a large, blended family.

Recapturing the magic of courtship is a crucial part of the healing process. Prioritize spending time together. Resurrect 'date night' and recapture the mystery and intensity you once had when you were first dating.

How to Date Your Mate

Far too many couples are lazy daters. They plan dates when it is convenient. They go on the same tired outings. They exert little to no effort and demonstrate no creativity in their planning.

If you are tired of settling for a monotonous dating life consider the following:

- **Variety is the spice of life (and dating)** – Simple dates to familiar places are fine, provided that you don't settle into a predictable routine. Keep things fresh by also planning more elaborate dates involving new experiences, detailed planning, and incorporating some element of mystery or surprise. To keep your date life fresh, include casual and formal dates, simple dates and elaborate dates, quick coffee dates and extended weekend getaways. Above all, make it fun!

- **Become a student of your partner** – A key to planning good dates is tailoring them to your partner's unique qualities. Learn your mate's likes and dislikes. Uncover his hopes and dreams. Explore her special talents and abilities. Find out if there's a skill or hobby your mate has always wanted to learn. This discovery process will give you insight into his or her passions and interests, which will help you to plan excellent dates that speak to your partner's heart. Additionally, it invites rich conversation, drawing you closer as you explore each other's hearts and souls.

- **Remove the stress** – Life is much more complicated than when we were kids. You can help your spouse relax and enjoy date night by handling all the logistics and preparations. Arrange childcare, print out directions that you may need, make dinner reservations, and take care of any details that will allow you both to more fully enjoy your time together.

- **Create anticipation** – When you plan a more elaborate date, build the anticipation. Send a card, or an e-mail inviting your husband or wife out on the date. You could even leave hints or clues every day or two over the course of the week. There is no formula, but you want to spark your mate's imagination and curiosity. Everyone enjoys being pursued. By building anticipation you can recapture that sense of pursuit that was so exhilarating when you were first dating.

- **Plan surprises** – A little mystery adds spark to a date. If your spouse enjoys being surprised, planning a mystery date could effectively demonstrate how much your value your spouse. The surprise could be as simple as an unexpected detour for dessert or as elaborate as an entire evening unfolding one event at a time.

Honor Each Other

Back when you were dating, you treated each other with respect, greeted each other warmly, and genuinely showed enthusiasm about the relationship. When one of you entered the room, you both lit up. It's time to recapture that sense of being treasured and honored.

- Husbands, act with chivalry *(open doors, allow her to go first whenever possible, give her your coat, drop her off at the door during bad weather, carry things for her)*

- Give the gift of respect[5] *(ask for his opinion, build her up in public around others, give extra*

---

[5] While men and women both desire respect, they generally prioritize it differently. As Dr. Emerson Eggerichs explores in *Love and Respect*, forced to choose between them, most men would rather be respected than loved and most women would rather be loved than respected.

weight to his perspective, thank her for sacrifices she makes for the family)

- *Communicate with excitement (greet each other warmly, show enthusiasm when talking texting, make time to enjoy each other's company)*

- Treat each other with kindness in public and private *(publicly affirm your mate, privately express hurts and concerns in a loving and sensitive way)*

- Listen intently *(mute the TV, turn off your game, put down your hobby and attentively listen)*

Our marriage – When Tammy and I were dating and even into the first year of our marriage, chivalry was a huge priority for me. But somewhere along the way, the distractions of blending a family, fueling a career, managing finances, and battling health complications caused much of that to drop off. Selfishness and laziness replaced that desire to honor her. When we began the process of renewing our marriage, I vowed to recapture that code of chivalry and honor her above myself. I still do it today and it has greatly enriched our marriage.

Honor is an ancient concept, but it's an essential part of maintaining a lasting renewal in your marriage.

Love must be sincere. Hate what is evil; cling to what is good. Be devoted to one another in love. Honor one another above yourselves. – Romans 12:9-10

The Importance of Sexual Intimacy

Sexual intimacy bonds a husband and wife physically, spiritually, and emotionally. Unfortunately, far too many marriages fail to experience genuine intimacy in their sex life, because they foolishly stampede toward the big finish without slowing down to fully enjoy each other.

Evidence suggests sexual activity creates a chemical bond between partners. According to researchers at the University of California, San Francisco, the hormone oxytocin has been "associated with the ability to maintain healthy interpersonal relationships and healthy psychological boundaries with other people."[6] Oxytocin is released during orgasm and begins creating an emotional bond. That bond intensifies as the couple continues to be intimate.

But there's more to building intimacy than just engaging in chemical maintenance through an exchange of fluids. A deeper level of passion, beyond achieving an orgasm, allows

---

[6] "Psychiatry" (July 1999 issue), authored by researchers Rebecca Turner, PhD, UCSF and Teresa McGuinness, MD, PhD, UCSF

a couple to bond at increasingly deeper levels both emotionally and spiritually. Read through the Song of Solomon. There are constant references to kissing, breasts, the lover's "gardens," and "eating the choicest fruits" from the "garden," "opening to each other," and being drenched by "myrrh." Woven throughout these erotic passages, you'll discover wise words about the power of love.

Place me like a seal over your heart, like a seal on your arm; for love is as strong as death, its jealousy unyielding as the grave. It burns like blazing fire, like a mighty flame. – Song of Solomon 8:6

Many waters cannot quench love; rivers cannot sweep it away. If one were to give all the wealth of one's house for love, it would be utterly scorned. – Song of Solomon 8:7

I am my beloved's and my beloved is mine. – Song of Solomon 6:3

Sexual intimacy means slowing down, taking your time, and reveling in the thrill of each other's time and attention. It means being vulnerable with each other. Use all of your senses. Smell one another's skin. Listen to what your lover enjoys and does not enjoy. Above all, focus on the journey of exploring, caressing, tasting, exciting, soothing, and loving. The destination is great, but stop and enjoy the roses (along with all of the other beautiful parts of your mate's "garden").

Dream Together

Dreaming is a wonderful way to unite behind a shared vision for the future. Tammy and I created a "Dream Book," but you could simply create a list of shared dreams that you both want to work toward to achieve. We first mentioned this in Chapter 7 as a potential activity during your first forty days of renewal. Many couples have lost hope of a bright future for their marriage. We recommend the dream book to help you start dreaming again. Whether you started one then or decide to start one now, dreaming together and planning your future is an important part of maintaining your marriage's freshness and focus. It's not a one-time activity, but an on-going conversation within your marriage regarding what your goals and dreams.

The following are some example goals:

- Places to visit (landmarks, cities, countries)
- Skills to learn (new language, gardening, cooking, dancing, a couple's sport like tennis)
- Experiences to have (pilgrimage, sky-diving, snorkeling, sailing)
- Volunteer/mission projects (local/global ministry, charity fundraising, church service)

- Projects around the house (start a garden, remodel the kitchen, create an outdoor space)

- Businesses to start (something that combines both of your talents and experiences)

- Vacations to take (cruise or resort, terrain or location, tour of certain areas)

- Events to attend (concerts, galas, festivals, games)

Make your list unique to your marriage. Some items may appeal to you while others appeal to your spouse, and some will excite you both. Selecting goals for your dream book creates an opportunity to learn more about your spouse and spend time in his or her world. Include dreams that don't appeal to you, but cater to your mate's interests. This act of mutual submission will deepen your appreciation for each other's uniqueness while opening you to activities you might otherwise avoid.

Create a plan to realize your dreams
What steps will you need to take to realize each dream? Are some of them a few years off while others need to happen soon? Some may require saving money. Others may require saving up vacation days. Still others will necessitate training and preparation (a long cross-country trek, a marathon, or detailed research).

Revisit your dreams every year and reflect on how close you are to realizing them and adjust your plans as needed. You may want to add new dreams and modify or remove others as your interests and circumstances change.

Make it happen

Choose an item on the list and make it happen! Start researching, saving money, getting in shape, whatever you need to do to put your plan in action. This dream book uniquely reflects your ongoing love story. Document the dreams you complete, including a description of how you completed each one. Include photographs and mementos to capture the heart of the memory. This description will serve as a lasting memory of the vibrant story that you and your soulmate have created together.

Leaving a Legacy

A lot of time, pain, and heartache have passed since that first date when Tammy and I lost track of time. But that doesn't mean the magic has to disappear. Every day offers us the opportunity to recapture romance. Never stop courting your mate. Make love passionately and vulnerably. Keep dreaming together and chasing those dreams as a team. Let this be the year you and your mate began a legacy of love and unwavering commitment that impacts your family for generations.

Chapter Ten Reflections

1. When was the last time that you and your mate went on a date without kids?

2. What are your most common obstacles/excuses for NOT dating your spouse?

3. What can you do to overcome those obstacles/excuses?

4. Commit to a consistent date night. Further, commit to investing time and thought into making your dates special. This doesn't have to be expensive, just thoughtful.

    a. When can you commit to having date night?

    b. What can you do to add variety to your dates?

5. Identify a few of your partner's interests that you could incorporate into future dates.

6. What steps can you take to reduce the stress surrounding date night (kid care, planning in advance, getting directions, etc.)?

7. What could you do to build anticipation for some of your dates?

8. Commit to deepen your love for each other.

   a. How can you how more honor in your marriage?

   b. What can you do to improve the quality of your sex life?

11

Prioritizing Your Marriage

Happily ever after is not a fairy tale. It's a choice.

Fawn Weaver

D URING THE PRE-FLIGHT PROTOCOL, flight attendants demonstrate a series of procedures that must be followed for your safety and the safety of others. One key instruction is given: "Put on your own oxygen mask first." In the event that oxygen masks are deployed, you should put your own oxygen mask on before helping a child seated next to you. *But what about "women and children first"?* While that's a good, chivalrous policy, it's a terrible idea in this situation. If you put your child's mask on first, you may pass out before getting your own mask on. If you put yours on first, then you will be conscious and able to assist the child beside you.

Your kids are important. Treat them with love and care. But they should not be your top priority. Your parents are important. Treat them with honor and love. But they should not be your top priority. The same goes for your extended family, your friends, your neighbors, and anyone else in your circle. Serving these people and honoring them is important, but should be a distant third on your list of priorities (yes, even your children).

Marriage is your most important earthly relationship. When you marry, the two of you become "one flesh." If you starve your marriage, you starve yourself. Nourishing your relationship and prioritizing your mate is one of the most important things you can do each day. The only thing more important, is your relationship with God.

"Put on your own oxygen mask first." This principle is realized through two supreme priorities. *First*, daily seek peace through an authentic walk with your Heavenly Father. *Second*, deepen and enrich your marriage.

Priority #1 – Your Spiritual Walk

If you don't eat, you won't have energy. If you don't fill up your car with gas, you can't drive it. Batteries run down. Fuel gets used up. Reserves get depleted. Energy of all kinds must be replenished. Your heart is no different.

Your ability to love your spouse and treat him or her with kindness and gentleness, or with any of the fruits of the spirit (Galatians 5:22-23) depends upon the quality and consistency of your spiritual life. If you do not regularly seek refreshment from your Heavenly Father, then your internal reserves will eventually run dry.

Your spouse is going to disappoint you. Miscommunication will happen and your needs will go unmet from time to time. When your spouse inevitably falls short of expectations, you can nag and complain or take your concerns to the Lord through prayer. Guess which one will be more successful for you? Your connection with God provides the oxygen you need to care for your spouse and for others. Prioritize accordingly.

Priority #2 – Your Relationship with your Spouse

Your second priority is not your kids. It's not your job, your social club, or your hobby. Your extended family was critically important in shaping who you are, but they aren't your second priority either. Your spouse – the person you pledged to love for the rest of your life – tops the list, second only to your Heavenly Father.

That might seem simple on the surface, but it comes down to *time* and *choices*. Honestly answer the following:

- In a given week, how often do you spend dedicated, one-on-one time with your spouse?
- Does your hobby take precedence over your mate?

- If you have the choice between what is convenient for you and what is convenient for your spouse, which do you tend to choose?

- Do you invest more energy in being successful at work or more energy in being a successful partner in your marriage?

- If you had to choose between doing something that blesses your mate vs doing something that blesses one of your kiddos or a close friend, which are you more likely to choose?

Every day, your choices reflect the priority you give your marriage. Like seasons, your circle of friends will change over time. Jobs will come and go. Your children will grow up and eventually move out (hopefully). Through it all, your husband or wife will be by your side. Don't take that for granted. Pursue your partner's heart with purpose and intensity.

Priority #3 – Your Family, Friends, and Everything Else

While relegating your children to third place may seem odd, this is actually the best gift you can give them. Their parents' healthy relationship and a strong marriage will impact every other relationship they have throughout their lives, including their own marriages.

The health of your marriage has a profound impact on your children. If you model respectful communication and conflict resolution with honor, your children will have more successful relationships. A strong marriage provides kids with confidence, comfort, and security. Perhaps most importantly, they need to know the proper order in the home. Have you ever met a child who has been raised to believe he is the center of his parent's world? Such a child has no perspective and no balance. Children need to know their parents' marriage is more important than catering to their every interest or whim.

Similarly, extended family must experience what Scripture describes as "leaving father and mother" and "cleaving" to your mate (Genesis 2:24, Matthew 19:5 and Ephesians 5:31). Leaving and cleaving expresses God's desire for the two of you to bond and create "one flesh." Your family of origin is important ("Honor your father and mother" – Exodus 20:12, Ephesians 6:2), but when you marry, you must detach from your original family and bond with your mate to create a new family.

Friends, church members, co-workers, and neighbors all fall into this third category. Loving them, investing in them, and even sacrificing for them is noble and encouraged. Yet connecting with these extended relationships must never take precedence over your marriage or your walk with God.

Love is like a Fire

FIRE IS AN AMAZING ELEMENT. Early on it is frail and unpredictable, capable of extinguishing quickly or expanding rapidly. In time it grows fierce and wild. Your relationship will go through phases and, like a fire, will take on different qualities and a different tempo at various times. Bruce Lee eloquently described the process of maturing love:

Love is like a friendship caught on fire. In the beginning a flame, very pretty, often hot and fierce, but still only light and flickering. As love grows older, our hearts mature and our love becomes as coals, deep-burning and unquenchable.

Some get discouraged when their relationship enters a new phase. They long for the sparks and the brightness of the flame they once experienced early in the relationship, but sparks do not provide sustainable warmth. The tinder and dry grass you use to start a fire create a bright and wild flame, which generates tremendous heat quickly, but also rapidly burns out. When you build a relationship primarily on sparks and quick-burning, hot flames, you cannot sustain this rhythm. In fact, such a relationship will eventually burn through the available fuel, leaving nothing but ash. Fortunately, God can work with that. He's done a lot more with a lot less.

The strength of your marital fire depends upon your priorities. The fuel for your relationship comes from the source – your Heavenly Father who loves you and knows your every need. Your second priority should be tending the fire, adding more lumber, blocking the wind, and moving the logs. Over time, these create hot coals that burn deep and provide sustainable heat.

Your Phoenix Marriage

Begun with the best of intentions, some marriages crumble, degrade, or burst into flames until there is nothing left but a pile of ash. **But where people see only doubt and despair, God sees hope and potential**. He refreshes and restores. Redeems and renews. Through Christ, we are made a new creation.

This means that anyone who belongs to Christ has become a new person. The old life is gone; a new life has begun! – II Corinthians 5:17 (NLT)

Your marriage can also be made **new**. Not just salvaged or repaired, but vibrant and stronger than ever. You can do more than survive – you can *thrive*. From the ashes of your demolished relationship, hope is born. The seeds of your new marriage are planted in fertile soil, nourished by the nutrient-rich ash. What appeared to be rubbish – the remnants of your suffering marriage – provide the starting point for your new life together. As you work to repair your communication, heal the broken places in each other's hearts, and rekindle your romance, your new marriage is birthed. Like the mythological phoenix, your renewed marriage emerges from the debris, spreads its wings, and soars.

God creates beauty out of ashes. He makes marriages out of messes. And He wants to work a miracle in yours.

Chapter Eleven Reflections

1. What practical steps can you take to improve your relationship with God?

2. In what ways can you prioritize your marriage more than you currently do?

3. How do you need to adjust the priority that you currently hold for your family, friends, and everything else (hobbies, work, etc.)?

4. What is currently holding you back from initiating or sustaining a renewal in your marriage? Identify practical steps for overcoming these obstacles.

Remember: Where people see only doubt and despair, God sees hope and potential. He refreshes and restores. Redeems and renews. Through Christ, we are made new.

A

Recommended Tools and Resources

Through re-building our own relationship and walking alongside other couples in renewing theirs, we have assembled a collection of tools, resources, and techniques. We hope you find them to be helpful in your journey as well.

Books (Enrichment)

- *The Love Dare* (2013) by Stephen and Alex Kendrick

    - Prescribes a daily "dare" to draw you closer together over a period of 40 days

- *Love & Respect*: *The Love She Most Desires, the Respect He Desperately Needs* (2004) by Emerson Eggerichs

    - Defines a useful set of tools and illustrations to help couples break the typical cycle of misunderstanding and miscommunication.

- *The Five Love Languages: How to Express Heartfelt Commitment to Your Mate* (1995) by Gary Chapman.

- Introduces a ground-breaking paradigm for understanding how your mate is wired and adapting your expression of love accordingly.

- *For Men Only: A straightforward guide to the inner lives of women* (2013), and *For Women Only: What you need to know about the inner lives of men* (2013), by Shaunti and Jeff Feldhahn

  - These two companion books are indispensable tools in understanding the thoughts of your mate. Through meticulous research and thorough surveys, the Feldhahns share wit, wisdom, and critical insight.

- *Intimate Encounters: A Practical Guide to Discovering the Secrets of a Really Great Marriage* (1994), by Dr David and Teresa Ferguson and Dr. Chris and Holly Thurman

  - This couple's study is packed with tools, techniques, scripture, stories, and insight into marriage and developing genuine intimacy.

Books (Re-building Trust)

- *Surviving an Affair* (2013), by Dr. Willard F. Harley, Jr. and Dr. Jennifer Harley Chalmers

  - Clarity, comfort, and compassion for those wounded by infidelity.

- – Provides guidance in rebuilding trust and restoring your marriage.

- *When Godly People Do Ungodly Things* (2003), Beth Moore

    - – Enlightening and inspirational, Moore divides her work into three basic sections: the Warning (spiritual attacks), the Watchman (protecting yourself), and the Way Home (recovering from moral failure).

Books (Spiritual)

- *Battlefield of the Mind: Winning the battle in your mind* (2002) by Joyce Meyer

    - – Sheds light on the spiritual warfare taking place in our lives and how the enemy battles for control of your thoughts.

- *The Screwtape Letters* (1942), C.S. Lewis

    - – A brilliant, satirical work of fiction that strives to provide a glimpse into the spiritual warfare that in constantly raging all around us.

- *When Godly People Do Ungodly Things (see above)*

Miscellaneous Resources

- *Simply Romantic Nights* (2008), FamilyLife Publishing

  - Improve your date nights through creativity, planning, thoughtful engagement, and intimacy-deepening fun. Twenty-four passionate date ideas (twelve for each of you), will enhance your emotional intimacy while making memories and enhancing sex.

- Stephen's Ministries – *www.stephensministries.org*

  - Offers faith-based mentoring through lay caregivers (Stephen Ministers) – to provide supportive and confidential, Christ-centered care to hurting people.

Check-ins (Recommended in Chapter 7)

- Love tank

  - Introduced in *Love & Respect* (Emerson Eggerichs), it provides a way to connect and gauge how loved your spouse feels.

  - Periodically throughout the day, you have a "tank check". On a scale of 1 to 10, how full is your partner's *love tank* (i.e. how loved does he or she feel)? Anything below a 7 warrants a discussion to understand the gap.

- Staff meetings

    - Recommended by David and Theresa Ferguson (The Great Commandment Ministries), staff meetings are a weekly activity that define a structured time period to discuss the week's events, take stock of how each other is feeling, pray over the relationship, and identify opportunities for improvement.

- Touch-base

    - The simplest type of check-in is the "touch-base." Take time out of your day to connect with your mate. The touch-base could occur via text message, email, or phone call. How is your husband or wife feeling? What can you do to help?

Social Media (Recommended in Chapter 7)

- Battleground Men – *Email-based ministry*

    - Daily e-mail encouragement focused on equipping men to be better husbands, fathers, and soldiers for Christ.

    - Currently available by invitation only. Email Chad Griffin at chad@battlegroundmen.com for more information.

- **Equip Your Marriage** - *EquipYourMarriage.com*
    - Weekly blog posts
    - Social media tips and encouragement
    - Weekly podcast
- Fierce Marriage – *www.fiercemarriage.com*
    - Blog
    - Social media tips and encouragement
    - Multimedia resources
- Husband Revolution – *www.husbandrevolution.com*
    - Blog for men
    - Social media tips and encouragement
    - Daily prayer
- Marriage Revolution - *www.marriagerevolution.com*
    - Licensed couples counseling
    - Events
    - Social media tips and encouragement
- Unveiled Wife – *www.unveiledwife.com*
    - Blog for women
    - Social media tips and encouragement
    - Daily prayer

B

Testimonies of Marriage Renewal

Testimony offers a powerful illustration of what is possible. It opens your mind to the potential existing within yourself and within your marriage.

Andrew Doan, MD, PhD and Julie Doan

Andrew Doan grew up in a verbally abusive home, leaving him with low self-esteem and an intense yearning for love and acceptance. He was an approval junkie and an ideal candidate to embrace addictive behaviors as an escape from his emotional pain.

From his book, *Hooked on Games*[7]:

> I was a mess, emotionally and spiritually. I was lost, angry, hateful, frustrated, and hurt. Above all, I had a deep need for love and acceptance. I was broken, and this behavior carried over into my marriage. I did not know how to be a kind and loving partner.

---

[7] Andrew P. Doan, MD, PhD, *Hooked on Games: The lure and cost of video game and Internet addiction*, FEP International, 2012

My wife Julie and I argued often and were unable to work as a team.[8]

He describes how he adopted the old pattern of verbal abuse he had learned as a child and berated his wife constantly. Stressed out at work, at home, and trying to cope with the difficulties of graduate school, Andrew sought an escape through video games. He writes:

> In video games, I found respect, acceptance, love, encouragement, challenge, ego boosts, and leadership opportunities. I had control over my video game avatars, toons, and profiles. I selected their physical features and other characteristics. I finally could look the way I envisioned. I felt godly in the games, and I tasted control and power.
>
> As an adult, I couldn't bully others in real life without serious consequences, so I turned to games played over the Internet to seek power and control over others. But as I dove deeper into video games, my real life was falling apart.[9]

Andrew's video game addiction continued for over nine years while simultaneously completing his MD/PhD and residency program. In addition to the massive amount of time necessary for medical school and then residency, he

---

[8] Doan, p114
[9] Doan, p115

would still manage to play forty to fifty hours of online games in a typical week. There was no time left for his wife or children. Some weeks he played even more, particularly during holidays and vacations when he should have been focused on his family.

In time, he changed into a cruel, unhealthy, and out of control version of himself. His addictive behavior transformed him mentally, physically, and spiritually. Perpetually irritated and constantly angry, he became abusive towards his wife and kids. He withdrew from family, friends, and colleagues, preferring the solitude and sense of power that video games offered.

As his severe verbal abuse intensified, his anger turned to fits of rage.

> I broke chairs, punched walls, and threw items around the house, yelling: "I hate you!", "You're holding me back!", "Why are you so needy?", and "Stop crying—you're so weak."[10]

Convinced she had married a monster, Julie secretly moved three thousand miles away, filed a restraining order, and petitioned for divorce and custody of the kids. Nearly ten years of abuse and neglect had taken its toll on their marriage and on Julie's own emotional and mental health.

---

[10] Doan, p119

Andrew describes his devastation and sense of isolation.

> During the height of my video game addiction, I had
> stopped calling my family or hanging out with
> friends. I was an agnostic with no faith and no
> guidance whatsoever. And yet, I remember one day
> lying on the floor crying, praying to any god that
> would listen to me. I prayed for help and for the
> return of my family.[11]

He began contemplating and even planning suicide.

> I had lost all of my friends, my wife, and my kids. My
> soul was empty. I had nothing. Eventually, after
> divorce attorneys and custody battles for the kids,
> my wife gave me a second chance but only with the
> understanding that I would start going to church
> with her.[12]

As a part of their renewal agreement, Julie required
Andrew to participate in a Bible study with her. What
started out as duty, turned into a critical turning point.
While reading *The Purpose Driven Life* by Rick Warren,
Andrew discovered he was created with a purpose.

Up to this point, he had been squandering his gifts, but
now he wanted to choose a path of purpose. In so doing, he

---

[11] Doan, p119
[12] Doan, p120

found the love and acceptance he had been seeking his entire life. Andrew writes:

> Finally, after over a decade of struggling and almost losing everything that mattered in my life, I found my way through God's guidance and discovered the path to recovery. I did not try to moderate my playing. I did not cut back. By God's grace, I stopped playing completely.[13]

As Andrew and Julie continued to invest in their marriage, healing took root and a peace and purpose encompassed their marriage. They began counseling other married couples, sharing hard-won insights and wisdom. They adopted a child from China and resolved to make up the precious time gaming had stolen from them. Recently, the Doan's celebrated 18 years of marriage together. Theirs is a love born of grit and determination.

Dr Andrew and Julie Doan founded Real Battle Ministries, an educational organization offering research, support and practical help for families in the digital age. They focus on technology overuse and video game addiction. Dr. Doan is the author of Hooked on Games: The lure and cost of video game and Internet addiction (2012).

---

[13] Doan, p123

Derek and Lisa Guyer

Lisa Guyer dreamt big dreams for her life. She would marry, have children, make priceless memories with her family, and live happily ever after. She and her husband Derek set out on the adventure together, but along the way, something went horribly wrong.

Derek and Lisa partnered with the owner of a horse ranch to develop a business offering therapeutic horse riding for adults and children with disabilities. They had always dreamed of having this kind of business, but as it grew, Derek had to be away from the ranch more and more. Unfortunately, this left Lisa alone with one other male worker to manage the daily business of providing horse riding therapy.

As Lisa writes on their blog, *Rise of the Home*:

> My co-worker and I continued on in our daily routines of helping clients and doing more riding lessons. We became close friends as we worked one-on-one for hours at a time. We talked about riding, our interests, and life in general. We soon became close enough that we began talking about the relationships that we were in and our pasts. Even in this, it was all very innocent in my mind. But, I was slowly opening the door for Satan to come into my life.

Relationships aren't destroyed in a day. Like the Casting Crowns' song *Slow Fade*, they erode and decay a day at a time. This was true for Lisa and Derek as well.

One day as Lisa and her co-worker were wrapping up a day of work, their shared familiarity tipped into something more intimate.

> Eventually, the day came when we said goodbye for the day, and something happened at this goodbye. Something changed. He gave me a look. There was an awkward silence. Then, he gave me a seemingly innocent kiss on the cheek. Satan had seen the open door and took full advantage of it.

From there, conversations ensued and the relationship quickly escalated. Lisa had opened herself up emotionally to another man and that closeness paved the way for an affair. Lisa describes how the relationship hardened her heart and poisoned the beautiful bond she had with Derek.

> Day after day, my heart got harder and harder. I began lying to Derek about when I would be at work. I lied about my pager being broken and being unable to call. I lied about why I was getting dressed up to go ride horses. I lied about everything. Our home fell apart. We began fighting when we never had fought before. I began resenting him. I began believing the lies that were being told to me. Satan, through my

co-worker, was filling my head with all of the things that Derek was doing wrong and how poorly he was treating me. I believed them and hated that Derek would treat me that way. No man would push me around! I even lied when Derek confronted me and asked if I was having an affair. The very idea that he would accuse me of that! Of course, I knew deep down in my heart that it was wrong and that he was right. But Satan quickly let that thought fly out the window.

Pain and grief piled up, surrounding their marriage, and suffocating the life out of their relationship. But the Lord wasn't finished with them yet, and He continued to pursue Lisa's heart. She became convicted of the necessity to confess to Derek and they began the long journey home to the Father and reconciliation.

Derek fully committed to the process of marriage renewal without hesitation. Lisa, on the other hand, still struggled with a heart that had become progressively hardened. It took time to soften her heart and become open to the changes that needed to be made. Fortunately, they were not alone in their struggle. The Spirit slowly eroded the hardness that had plagued Lisa's heart. During this time, Derek stayed committed and patient even while being repeatedly rejected by his bride. Eventually, Lisa stepped in alongside Derek to work together in restoring their marriage. They invested time and energy in building their communication skills and sharing openly in a raw, authentic way. They prioritized serving one another. Most of all, they submitted to a process of waiting on the Lord and allowing His timing to heal, restore, and empower them to reach their full purpose as a couple.

Derek attributes the redemption of their marriage to a solid faith in Jesus. As he describes it, one can't help but notice the phoenix-esque imagery he uses when talking about the renewal of their marriage and home.

> We have risen from the ashes of death and destruction and have a home that honors God. We still fall, but we are on the rise and all thanks to the blood of Jesus. To save our marriage, we looked to the "author and perfecter of our faith, who for the joy that was set before him, endured the cross, despising the shame" and now he sat down at the right hand of the throne of God to mediate for us. Jesus showed us how to love one another, by loving us and giving himself up for us. That's how we saved our marriage and our home, and began to rise. We are products of an amazing plan. We are redeemed.

Derek and Lisa Guyer celebrated twelve years of marriage earlier this year. They have six beautiful children and a deep commitment to Christ and one another. They share a passion for expressing the redemptive love of their Heavenly Father with others.

Derek and Lisa Guyer serve as marriage mentors and writers. They share relationship wisdom and insight through their website, Rise of the Home – www.riseofthehome.com

Chad and Amy Griffin

Chad Griffin grew up in a small town in south Texas. He lived a typical, uneventful childhood. He regularly attended church, but didn't really let it penetrate his heart or change his life. An avid athlete and self-proclaimed womanizer, he enjoyed the "thrill of the chase" and made it a personal goal to make out with as many girls as he could in school. Throughout his high school and college career, Chad loved three things: sports, women, and himself. He thought nothing of jumping from girl or girl or even stringing several of them along at the same time.

In college, Chad's "mad skillz" as a "playa" stopped short when he met an angel named Amy. Initially, she wanted nothing to do with him due to his reputation on campus. Eventually, Chad's persistence and sincerity won her over, and they began to date. Nine months later they were engaged. Eighteen months after that, they were married. And they lived happily ever after...*for a few months*.

Before their one year anniversary, Chad committed adultery. Through counseling and the grace of the Lord, Amy forgave him.

For the next fourteen years, Chad battled with lust and continued to slip into his old patterns. From inappropriate emails, hugs, and conversations, to being physically involved with three to four women at a time, he allowed the devil to wreak havoc on his life. Only this time, he kept it hidden from Amy.

Chad's demons intensified, and he fell into lust with a woman with whom he was prepared to start a new life with. He and Amy talked about divorce, but Chad never revealed his recent escapades. Finally, the pressure became too much for him to bear. As Chad describes it:

> I'd like to say there was a miraculous sign or event from God that turned things around. A prophetic word or voice from Heaven, but nothing like that occurred. Conviction from the Holy Spirit and the thought of my children hating their daddy caused my mistress and me to grow apart. Days of no contact turned into weeks, which turned into months. I was becoming a husband again, a father. Amy had no idea of any of these infidelities, and I planned to carry this burden to my grave.

At the urging of an old friend, Chad embarked upon a six-day Faith Quest through Fellowship of the Sword. During that quest, God profoundly took hold of. Near the end of the quest, he wrote a letter to Amy confessing *everything*, including names of every woman he'd been emotionally or physically unfaithful with over the previous 14 years. When he returned home, he handed Amy the letter. That Sunday night in May 2011, he became a free man, deciding never to be chained by lies or deceit again.

While Chad was feeling relief and freedom, Amy was grappling with devastation:

> I was angry and upset. My heart was crushed. My mind began spinning with questions of what this means for us as a couple and as a family. It was so overwhelming. I had never been hurt so badly, and I couldn't make sense of it all. One thing I did know was that I was furious. I was furious at Chad but I was also furious at Satan. Even with all of my anger, I knew in my heart that we weren't going to get divorced. I loved Chad and I knew that somehow we would work through it.

Rebuilding and renewing their relationship was difficult, but as Amy describes it, there simply was not another option in her mind "I refused to let the devil have this marriage," she explains. Through counseling, prayer, and an army of supportive believers, they knit their fragile relationship into a strong and vital marriage.

Paramount in their renewed marriage is a dependence upon God. They pray together every night, even if one of them is out of town. Quiet time with The Father is an essential, daily activity for them individually as well as together. They describe their relationship with God as being stronger, both individually and also as a couple.

Another key to their successful renewal has been investing in their friendship. Date night with no kids is a priority for them to keep the fires burning. Their communication is open and real. Amy highlights the importance of frequent contact: "We talk a lot now. Several times a day, throughout the day, we talk about big things and little things. It really makes the day better when you have that on-going connection with your best friend."

Chad and Amy Griffin are a dynamic couple. Their perseverance has paid off for their marriage and their family. Active in their local church and in mission work in Vietnam and Uganda, they are fully committed to Christ and each other. When asked how they made it past the pain and into the bright future that they enjoy now, Amy said simply, "God is the only reason we are married today. God put the forgiveness in me. He's the reason we were able to overcome."

Chad Griffin is the founder of The Battleground Men's Ministry, an e-mail based ministry that equips and encourages men all around the world as soldiers of Christ. He is a disciple, mentor, and public speaker with a passion for equipping men to fulfill their calling in Christ.

About the Author

KYLE GABHART IS A DEVOTED HUSBAND AND FATHER OF SIX. He is also an author, public speaker, and entrepreneur. In February 2014, he and his wife Tammy, founded *EquipYourMarriage.com*, a faith-based ministry dedicated to empowering, equipping, and restoring marriages. The Gabhart's produce a veritable marriage toolbox through challenging blog posts, encouraging tweets, inspiring images, and instructional audio and video content. When not engaged in marriage ministry, Kyle is an avid soccer player and board game enthusiast, but he prides himself on being a constant embarrassment to his children.

About Equip Your Marriage Ministries

GOD IS LEADING A MOVEMENT OF REVIVAL AMONGST MARRIAGES. He is calling for renewal and restoration. Equip Your Marriage (EYM) Ministries is one small piece of that bigger Kingdom picture. Available at *EquipYourMarriage.com* as well as on Facebook, Twitter, Pinterest, and Youtube, EYM ministries offers resources to equip and empower marriages to reach their full potential in Christ.

Perspectives on *The Phoenix Marriage*

"Kyle and Tammy have packed this book with practical application and solid biblical guidance. The Phoenix Marriage lays out a crystal clear roadmap for marriage renewal. I believe Christian marriages should be the model of marriage in the world. What a powerful testimony and tool to reach people!"

- Rob Ketterling, Lead Pastor
River Valley Church

"In a world full of quitters, it takes true courage to commit to marriage renewal. If you want a field manual for restoring your relationship, get *The Phoenix Marriage"*

- Tony Jeary
The RESULTS Guy™

"Kyle and Tammy step out of the droves of repaired marriages and share a beautiful testimony of God's redemptive love."

- Carlotta Dyan Dejewski
RenovatingTheTemple.com

"Excellent resource! I only wish this book had been published five years ago when my wife and I began the process of renewing our own marriage."

- Chris B., Husband and Father.
Marriage restored in 2009.

"Kyle is a man on a mission to share God's desire and plan for marriage restoration with as many couples as will listen. His story will encourage you. His passion will inspire you. And, the tools he has learned and applied will give you a plan to follow in your own marriage."

- Hans Molegraaf
Marriage Revolution

13396061R10103

Made in the USA
Lexington, KY
31 October 2018